THEY CALL ME PASTOR

AMONG OTHER THINGS

NELSON COFFMAN

Five
Stones
Press

COPYRIGHT

CONTENTS

DEDICATION

I dedicate this book to the countless pastors and ministry leaders who ever felt like giving up and quitting the ministry. I also dedicate this book to my wonderful wife Karen of 49 years, who has faithfully supported me through every difficult and challenging season of my life and ministry. Lastly, I dedicate this book to my three children, Kasey, Justin, and Kirk, who have given their lives in service to the Lord. I pray this book will help them through the challenging journey called ministry.

ENDORSEMENTS

In this book you hold in your hand may very well be the difference between finishing well and failing miserably.

I have walked with Pastor Nelson Coffman for over 25 years. If anyone has the right to write this type of book, it is him. You will find in this book an honest approach to not only surviving difficult seasons but also how to maintain an intimate private relationship with Jesus who is the Head of the Church.

Read this book like your life depended upon it. You will soon see this writing is filled with wisdom in how to stay out of the pitfalls that are too often contributed to leaders who have been captured by the identity of ministry and less about the relationship with Christ. You will see not only the pitfalls of human mistakes but also the traps the devil sets for those who are distracted by the external perceptions of ministry.

There is something in this book for the novice pastor but also the seasoned veteran. Threaded throughout the pages of this book is a continual admonition, that no matter what season or what people may say, one thing is constant which is God's love and purpose for you personally.

Kerry Kirkwood
Senior Pastor
Trinity Fellowship Church
Tyler, TX

Wisdom gained from others' experiences is like finding treasure on the surface that someone spent years digging for. Pastor Nelson has learned many valuable lessons on leadership and ministry, and sharing these lessons with us is priceless. May you be inspired and protected by the wisdom in this book.

Kody Hughes
The Heights Church
Cleburne, TX

How I wish there had been a class in the seminary that taught the truths laid out in this book. Ministry is tough and I know of no other book that will help a pastor or ministry leader more than this one as they walk through the mine field of ministry.

You will relate to much of it, and I believe, learn how to navigate the daily path of pastoral ministry from all of it.

So, read this book expecting God to give you practical tools to walk with as you fulfill His call on your life.

Olen Griffing
Pastor Shady Grove Church (Retired)
Grand Prairie, TX

Thank you, Pastor Nelson, for the honor of reading *They Call Me Pastor*. It reads like more than one book, since each chapter is so loaded with encouragement - for leaders in ministry - that they could also be published as mini-books. May our Lord continue using your writings to empower His people.

Alan Latta
Generations Church
Granbury,TX

They Call Me Pastor … Among Other Things is one of the most down to earth practical survival guides for pastors, I have read. I highly recommend it to all pastors, especially those who are starting or feel called to the ministry. I wish I would have had this book when I started in the ministry!

The writing style is delightful and easy reading, while the content is very helpful to those in ministry. I love this book.

D. Ray Miller

Pastored eight churches in two states over forty-five years. Served in Radio & TV ministry, Evangelist and Missions.

As a fellow pastor, I'm discerning about the leaders who truly influence my own leadership journey. Nelson stands out among them. His credibility is well-earned—he fearlessly addresses the daily challenges faced by pastors. His book combines inspiration and wit, offering practical guidance drawn not only from his personal experiences but also from those around him. These are leaders I know personally, individuals who have rightfully earned their place at the discussion table on church-related matters. Experience, after all, is the key to valuable advice. Like a seasoned traveler, Nelson provides direction based on where he's been. His book serves as an essential guide—an almost survival manual—for church leadership. It's a compelling read!

Ed Hearld
Victory Church
Bloomington, IL

THEY CALL ME PASTOR

AMONG OTHER THINGS

COPYRIGHT

INTRODUCTION

ANSWERING THE CALL

You have decided to answer God's call to pastoral ministry. Perhaps it is to birth a church, take the pastorate of an existing church, or to develop and lead a para-church ministry. I want you to know the Lord is proud of you; the world needs you and the church is desperate to find you whether they know it or not.

I have some good news and some bad news for you.

First, the bad news. An article titled Statistics on Pastors by Dr. Richard J. Krejcir states that research from Barna, Focus on the Family, and Fuller Seminary, shows that 1500 pastors leave the ministry each month due to moral failure, spiritual burnout, or contention in their churches. Fifty percent of pastors' marriages end in divorce. Seventy percent of pastors constantly fight depression and eighty percent of pastors feel unqualified and discouraged. As well, eighty percent Bible school graduates entering the ministry leave within five years.

This means the odds are stacked against us and a great percentage of us will fail at being a pastor. A great percentage of us will not achieve our goals or be successful in ministry. A large percentage will go through seasons of depression, doubt, and unbelief. Some may suffer great disappointment at the thought of failure, feeling like we've lost God's will for our life, all because we answered the call into pastoral ministry. Which, by the way, is not a guarantee that we'll be successful in ministry. That's the bad news.

As written in *The Chronicles of Leroy**, "Answering the call to ministry is a wonderful conversation until you hang up!"

The good news is this book will help keep us from hanging up and even more good news is we now have a survival guide!

I believe this book will help us stay engaged in the work of the ministry, beat the odds, and finish well the race we have been called to run. This book will also help us navigate through the difficult seasons of church life, ministry and leadership development. This guide will also help us navigate through the challenges of pastoral ministry and the people-problems that come with it. Hopefully, this book will help us survive the attacks that come from the enemy and well-meaning people we love and care about.

The best news of all is this: the One on the other end of

---

* Reference the Appendix - *The Chronicles of Leroy*

the line is for us, not against us. Never forget the Lord has confidence in us or he would not have dialed up our number.

Please understand this is not a book to help grow a mega church. The purpose of this book is to help us survive building a church, no matter what the size. The same is true if we are building a ministry. There are plenty of books available that give sound advice for growing the size of a church or ministry. I encourage reading them, but this book is different. It's a survival guide.

Though not designed to be a strategy for church growth, there are principles laid out within these chapters that will produce a healthy, growing church and a successful ministry. Contained within these pages are also wise insights from pastors who have learned the hard way, so we don't have to.

Navigation is the process of accurately ascertaining one's position, then planning and following a route. I hope what's shared here will encourage us through the tough seasons and navigate through the challenges all pastors and ministry leaders face. Let's get started.

ONE
THEY CALL ME A PASTOR
NAVIGATING THROUGH YOUR DECISION TO ANSWER THE CALL

Pastors and ministry leaders, the best advice I can give is the advice my pastor gave me at the first Bible College I attended in 1986. It came from Pastor Olen Griffing, my pastor of over 36 years. He said to a group of us, "If you can be anything but a pastor, be it!" I wholeheartedly agree. If there are any other vocational options or career choices please consider them carefully. Pastoral ministry is a tough road to travel.

This is true not just because of the attacks that come from the demonic realm, but because we are in the people business. When we are in the people business, we face the same challenges every leader in the Old and New Testament had to face from Moses to Jesus, from Joshua to Paul.

Pastor Olen likened ministry to Forrest Gump's take on the shrimping business. After numerous failures, Forrest exclaimed "Shrimppping is tough!" Pastoral ministry, as well as leading any ministry, is tough. The reason it's tough is that we're in the people business. As a well-known pastor once stated, "Pastoring a church would be great if it wasn't for the people."

Pastor Olen also stated that if we can't be anything but a pastor, it's a wonderful life. Meaning, that if we can't give our life away to any other thing, because we desire God's call above all else, then it truly is a wonderful life. We will be glad we picked up the phone and answered the call.

Pastors and ministry leaders settle the issue. I'm not saying we can't do anything else alongside pastoral ministry. Many men and women have answered the call to ministry and have full-time jobs alongside their callings. I'm just saying we can have only one priority.

The wisdom of Leroy tells us in *The Chronicles of Leroy*, "Ministry can be a juggling act in this circus called life."

I recall with clarity my early days in pastoral ministry: juggling the demands of being a full-time pastor, running a construction company and attending Bible college – all at the same time. On top of that, I was striving to be a devoted husband and father to three young kids. It was an incredible juggling act, each day a whirlwind of challenges and commitments.

There may be seasons when we feel our life is a juggling act of trying to be all the things everyone dependent upon us needs us to be. I encourage setting our heart on being, not just doing. I repeat: set our heart on being, not just doing. Start every day in the Lord's presence. Spend time with Him in communion, listening to His voice, meditating on His word as the son or daughter He has called us to be.

King David declared in Psalms 5:3, "Listen to my voice in the morning, Lord. Each morning, I bring my requests to you and wait expectantly." NLT

If we begin each day in the Lord's presence, we will discover Him orchestrating our day. We will find that our day goes better, and we accomplish far more than we expected. When we focus on His business, He will take care of our business. That is a bold thing to say, but just try it. God is the perfect logistics manager and has a knack for removing the little issues that shift our focus from His business. That doesn't mean we don't have to think about those things and make wise decisions. It just means that we refuse to let them distract us from being about our Father's business.

Choose a time and place to meet with the Lord. Show up at that same time and location every day to experience how powerful the Lord is leading and directing our life, especially during hard seasons. It is there that we experience an open window to heaven where our questions receive answers. We will receive revelation from the Lord and confidence in decision making. It is the place where we discern what is of the Spirit and what is of the flesh, what is of God and what is of the demonic realm. It is there that messages for our congregations will flow.

A great pastor friend of mine once observed, "The reason pastors wear out is that they are serving up meals Jesus never ordered!" Once a place of intimacy with the

Lord is found, we will never wear out. In this place, revelation from God's Word ignites sermons to become more than statements of fact, but illuminations from on high. These daily special times with the Lord are where He makes Himself known to us and confirms His Word. These private times with God are what we need to stand on when our congregations turn from gentle sheep into ravenous wolves. There can be seasons where congregations turn from being a loving and supportive flock into an angry mob, ready to lynch us. They may even call us names other than pastor. It is during these times that all we have to brace ourselves with is what the Lord has told us.

All we have to hold on to when the storm rages is what the Lord has spoken to us in our quiet time. Just as when Paul was in the middle of a raging storm and the word of the Lord came to him.

Acts 27:22 -24 "But take courage! None of you will lose your lives, even though the ship will go down. For last night, an angel of the Lord to whom I belong and whom I serve stood beside me. And He said, 'Don't be afraid, Paul, for you will surely stand trial before Caesar! What's more, God in His goodness has granted safety to everyone sailing with you.'" NLT

Find the daily place of prayer and communion with the Lord. Keep that rendezvous every day. Allow the Lord, through prayer and seeking, to answer questions and give us direction. The best counsel I can give on this is: don't leave that place of prayer until the conversation is finished.

Leroy says in *The Chronicles of Leroy*, "Sweating bullets in prayer is never wasted ammunition."

The question we must answer, as did I, is this: Can I be anything but a pastor? For me, the answer was clear that the Lord had called me to be a pastor. As I look back on my 38 years of ministry, I cannot imagine being anything else. I have seen the Lord do amazing things throughout my life. I would not have chosen any other calling than being a pastor. Hopefully, this book will help each of us survive the various other things we are called, other than *pastor*.

This is a good place for me to explain why I named this book *They Call Me Pastor…Among Other Things.* It's not only because when we're pastoring a small church or leading a small para-church ministry that we wear so many different hats. We are the primary leader of the ministry, the key speaker, counselor, motivator, secretary, and maintenance person. Not to mention the CEO of the organization and president of the corporation. Did I leave any hats out? I think I did because we still need to be a good spouse, parent and community liaison. Yes, we wear many hats.

The thought behind the title is also that people often talk about us in terms other than pastor. We are called many things, some good and some bad. Many of these names are dishonorable to our position and do not represent who we want to be. As well, many of the names we are called are honorable to our position and exactly who we want to be.

I have been called pastor, wonderful brother, compassionate leader, and encouraging speaker. These same people have called me uncaring, controlling, asinine,

long-winded, redundant, boring, and sinful. Thus, the title
They Call Me Pastor…Among Other Things.

These names, along with many others, most likely applied to me at various times in the life of my ministry. At least they did from some people's perspective. Being called something other than *pastor* can be very disheartening and make us want to quit, especially when we passionately care about the people we're called to minister to.

I did my best to not be boring or long-winded, knowing it has never been in my heart to come across as controlling or asinine. As far as being called sinful, there was a time in my ministry that I felt like a miserable failure. I was a Christian who desperately needed God's grace and mercy.

Name calling may be justified. Though it may be debated by pride, acknowledged, and repented of, it's not a reason to quit. If we will not give up, one day it will be said to us by those who our ministry touches," Pastor, I am so glad you never gave up".

TWO
THEY CALL ME SUCCESSFUL?
NAVIGATING THROUGH THE CHALLENGES OF FINDING SUCCESS IN MINISTRY

Notice the question mark in the title of this chapter. I believe it's important for any pastor or ministry leader to define success. What do we believe is a successful church or ministry? How do we define success? What is our definition of success? Please take a moment to think about the question. The reason this is so important is that we will have seasons in our ministry where we do not feel successful. We can find ourselves depressed and ready to give up during these times.

As a pastor or ministry leader, our definition of success is unique to us. Our definition of success may not look like someone else's definition. I submit that if our definition is based solely on someone else's definition, it will set us up for failure. I urge seeking the Lord and allowing Him to speak to our heart about our success through His eyes. How would the Lord define our success as a leader? How would

He define our church or ministry's success? What is success in the eyes of the Lord? If we are unsuccessful in His eyes, are we successful?

Therefore, we must define success. If our definition of success revolves around the number of people attending and supporting our ministry and we do not experience the growth or support that we expected, we will not feel successful. As wonderful as growth and large numbers of people who are supporting our ministry are, that definition of success may or may not be how God defines success for us. It's important for us to have the Lord impart into our heart His definition of success for us and the work He's called us to. I encourage defining success by that definition alone.

I define my success as a pastor by seeing people come into the fullness of God's calling and purpose for their lives. For me, when I see people using their giftings to glorify God, engaged in service to the Lord in the church or in the marketplace, when I see them walking in the very purpose for which God created them, that's success. That's when I feel successful. When I see people walking out their prophetic destiny and stepping into the things God has spoken over them prophetically, that's when I feel successful as a pastor. At Harvest Hill Church, the majority of our church body is engaged in ministry, and some are serving in multiple areas of ministry. Many are serving in the church and the marketplace.

I also find remarkable success with church growth, salvations, water baptisms, people coming into the fullness of the Holy Spirit, missions, benevolence ministry to the poor, evangelism, and everything else a life-giving church should be doing. However, what the Lord has placed on my heart is to define success by people coming to the fullness of God's calling, purpose, and prophetic destiny for their lives. What does God say that looks like for you?

Not every pastor is called to have a mega church, but we are called to have a successful church and a successful ministry. Mega church leaders have unique giftings from God to accomplish their calling and I admire them. However, we can all have successful churches and ministries when we define success the way the Lord defines it: walking in our callings. The Lord never calls us to failure, but to success. I encourage seeking the Lord and ask Him to give His definition of success for us and our church or ministry.

3 John 1:2 "Beloved, I pray that you may prosper in all things and be in health, just as your soul prospers." NKJV

As we read in *The Chronicles of Leroy*, "Size matters, the size of your vision, the size of your faith, the size of your obedience, and the size of your trust."

I encourage allowing God to define our success. As we navigate through difficult seasons of ministry, our success will be based upon what the Lord has said, not on our feelings or other's opinions. As leaders if we don't define success, other people's opinions of success will define us. My prayer is that we would allow the Lord to define our success so that on the day we stand before Him, it is the Lord who will call us successful.

THREE
THEY CALL ME PURPOSE DRIVEN

NAVIGATING THE CHALLENGES OF A PURPOSE DRIVEN MINISTRY

It is said the road of life is full of flattened squirrels that couldn't make a decision. This is true of pastors and ministry leaders who can't, or won't, make decisions that set them on course for God's purposes. We can end up flattened by our circumstances in the middle of a road going nowhere.

My fellow ministers, it is vital for us to slow our busy lives down long enough to examine exactly what God's purpose is for our life and ministry. In those slow down moments, God can make things known to us and we can adjust where needed. The Lord can help us see what we have yet to see and hear what we need to hear. The Lord can fine tune our fiddle, so to speak, if our fiddle is out of tune. If our life is not in tune with the will, plan, and purpose of God, I suggest spending some time alone with the Lord until it gets in tune. Call it a sabbatical or call it time off. Call it a vacation if need be.

Without question, this is one of the most important things we can do as we prepare for each season of our life. He can bring adjustments needed for the success we're striving to achieve. That way, we won't be as confused as a squirrel in the middle of the road, about to be flattened by a truck. Nor will we be living with stress and anxiousness.

Isaiah 48:17 "This is what the Lord says - your Redeemer, the Holy One of Israel: 'I am the Lord your God, who teaches you what is good for you and leads you along the paths you should follow.'" NLT

I encourage getting alone with God, so we run with purpose. Often, the very reason we are not experiencing the success we hope for is because we have gotten off track with God's purpose for our life and ministry.

I once took a three-month sabbatical. The main thing I came away with was a sense of urgency regarding my purpose. It was like a constant Holy Spirit burden. I don't know how else to explain this urgency of purpose, this constant reminder from the Holy Spirit concerning my purpose. Then I realized it wasn't guilt or conviction, but a prompting from the Holy Spirit giving me a clear purpose to run.

Has the Holy Spirit ever put in your heart a sense of urgency about something to do, to accomplish, or engage in or maybe something to do for someone or to say to someone? Just an urgency in our heart and mind to act! It's like when we know our anniversary is on Wednesday, or is it Tuesday? All we can think about is that we need to get a card. That was the urgency I felt while on sabbatical concerning my purpose.

During my sabbatical, the Holy Spirit confirmed to me I have a purpose on this earth, and I needed to be about what God was calling me to do because there is no time to waste. Writing this book has a lot to do with that sense of urgency.

Do you feel the clock ticking? Is there an urgency of purpose for what the Lord has called you to do? If not, why not? My suggestion is to evaluate yourself in each season of life. If you don't know your purpose, you need to discover it. Determine that if your purpose is lying dormant, you need to revive it. If you're not pursuing it, you need to start there. There is no time to waste.

Paul states in 1 Corinthians 9:25-26 "All athletes are disciplined in their training. They do it to win a prize that will fade away, but we do it for an eternal prize. So, I run with purpose every step. I am not just shadowboxing." NLT

History tells us this passage is a metaphor taken from runners in a race, exerting themselves, striving hard to perform with excellence and to win. This word occurs in Greek writings denoting to endure extreme peril, which requires the exertion of all one's effort to overcome.

I think most pastors and ministry leaders have a deep sense of purpose for what God has called them to do. However, I also understand the need they have to communicate to those whom God has called alongside them to have a sense of purpose as well. The bottom line is this: we can't do it by ourselves, and we need those people who God has called alongside us to run with purpose as well. Perhaps this is the greatest challenge we face as leaders of those people.

My hope is this chapter will give us insights to share with those people that they may run with purpose as well. Purpose is defined as certainty coming from the root word meaning *hidden*. We run with a sense of certainty, not something hidden. Paul's exhortation is that we are to run this race with purpose. It's the idea of giving all our strength to obtain something, regardless of the challenges faced in order to win.

There is a purpose for being in this race called life. I know so many Christians, and even pastors, who have never captured the concept that they are created for purpose. God has called and chosen them for His purpose. Sadly, the fruit of that lack of understanding is often no desire to discover their purpose, yet alone pursue it. Many, like Jonah, run from their calling.

The concept that the Lord has a purpose for His created beings is foreign to them, so they go through their entire life with no sense of real purpose. Life becomes a mundane, day-to-day chore, striving from one problem to the next, enduring until it's over. They are living from tragedy to tragedy, event to event, promotion to promotion, vacation to vacation, with retirement being their driving force.

Their philosophy of life includes getting out of bed, going to work, spending money, retiring, and dying. Now you may not be one of these people, but I know ministers who have this concept of life and the only hope they have, is to discover their purpose so that when they stand before God, He says, "Well done good and faithful servant," not "What were you thinking?"

We must have in the fabric of our belief system the understanding that we are created, called, and chosen for purpose, so that the people we are leading will develop that truth in the fabric of their belief system. When this happens, they will eagerly come alongside us in the work of the ministry that God has called us to.

I'm reminded of the story about the young man who wanted to become a lawyer. He goes to his pastor and tells him he wants to become a lawyer.

The pastor says, "Well, that's a good idea, but what then?"

The young man says, "Well, I guess I'll go to law school and get my degree."

The old pastor says, "Well, what then?"

The young man says, "I guess I will join a law firm."

The old pastor says, "Well, what then?"

The young man says, "Well, I guess I will rise to the top and become a partner in the firm."

The old pastor says, "Well, what then?"

The young man says, "Well, I guess I will retire a rich man."

The old pastor says, "Well, what then?"

And the young man says, "Well, I guess I will die."

The old pastor says "Well, what then?"

The moral of the story is that we can spend our whole life achieving what we believe is success, only to stand before the Lord unsuccessful. Let me lay a foundation from God's Word that we and those called alongside us can build our futures on.

First, we're created for purpose.

Eph 2:10 "For we are His workmanship, created in Christ Jesus for good works, which God prepared beforehand that we should walk in them." NKJV

That's my favorite scripture in the whole Bible. We are His workmanship. Your translation may say *His masterpiece*. It's the Greek word *poima*, where we get the word poem. Our lives are the poem of God, written before the world began, created in Christ for good works.

Second, we're called for purpose.

Rom 8:28 "And we know that God causes everything to work together for the good of those who love God and are called according to His purpose for them." NKJV

We should never separate things working together for our good from our purpose. Never separate all things working for your good from accomplishing God's purpose for your life. As Christians, we like to quote that scripture when things are going terribly wrong in our lives, expecting and believing that God will somehow work it out for our good. I believe we can and should believe and even expect God to work things for our good. However, I don't believe we can expect God to work things out for good if there is no love for God or answering the call to His purpose.

Last, we're chosen for purpose.

John 15:16 "You did not choose me, but I chose you and appointed you that you should go and bear fruit, and that your fruit should remain, that whatever you ask the Father in My name He may give you." NKJV

I pray this truth resonates in our hearts to a depth that the trajectory of our life is forever altered. We are created, called, and chosen for purpose. The whole concept of being chosen astonishes me. I am someone who likes to watch people. Watching people is interesting to me. I've traveled around the US and 11 countries watching people from small towns to large cities. I like to observe people from diverse backgrounds, cultures, and religions. All people have eyes, ears, and noses. They walk, talk and have blood running through their veins. They all have a mind and the ability to think and to reason. Each one has feelings and emotions like happiness, sadness and even anger. People feel sorrow and joy and all have problems and issues to deal with. People are alike, with one exception.

Do you know what that one exception is? Some are chosen. We are chosen. There is one thing and only one thing that makes us unique … we are chosen.

2 Thessalonians 2:13 "But we are bound to give thanks to God always for you, brethren, beloved by the Lord, because God from the beginning chose you for salvation through sanctification by the Spirit and belief in truth." NKJV

Ephesians 1:4 "Just as He chose us in Him before the foundation of the world, that we should be holy and without blame before Him in love." NKJV

1 Peter 2:9 "But you are a chosen generation, a royal priesthood, a holy nation, His own special people, that you

may proclaim the praises of Him who called you out of darkness into His marvelous light." NKJV

I pray we establish this in the fabric of our belief system. It means some are chosen, and some are not. So, the question arises, why? For what purpose have we been chosen? It's amazing that we have been created, called, and chosen for God's purpose. The goodness of God in showing us His purpose for our lives through scripture is amazing. Who are we that God would choose us to begin with? Who are we that God would reveal to us His purposes for choosing us? The whole concept is just astonishing!

Do you know how many people have lived on this earth? The estimate is over 100 billion. Obviously, there's no way to know for sure, but what if that number is accurate? Out of possibly 100 billion people, only some were chosen. Only a percentage were chosen by God for His purposes.

Jesus said in Matthew 7:14, "But the gateway to life is very narrow and the road is difficult, and only a few ever find it." NLT

You and I are born again, spirit-filled Christians, sons and daughters of the most high God, we are the chosen few. Our destiny is heaven, and our purpose is revealed on this earth. So, the question arises, can we be robbed of God's purposes on this earth? The answer is YES! We must beware of "purpose thieves", the thieves who rob us of God's purposes for our life.

To think we can be robbed of God's purposes is overwhelming. It may not be overwhelming right now, but that day will come, as in the story of the young lawyer and the old pastor asking him what then.

The first purpose thief is the devil, the deceiver, Satan, and the demonic forces that are set against us, scheme against us, plot our demise, and wrestle against us according to the book of Ephesians.

Ephesians 6:12 "For we do not wrestle against flesh and blood, but against principalities, against powers, against rulers of the darkness of this age, against spiritual hosts of wickedness in the heavenly places." NKJV

So, the number one purpose thief is the devil.

Why has there has been such an attack on our life and a barrage of attacks on our marriage, family, finances, health and ministry since we became a Christian? Why has there been such an attack on our mind and emotions, robbing us of joy, peace, self-worth, value, and self-confidence and an ongoing attack to get us down and depressed? The enemy's strategy is to rob us of our victory over sin and keep us bound up in doubt and unbelief for one and only one reason, our purpose!

Satan doesn't want our marriages, families, ministries, finances or any other areas of our life blessed. Satan doesn't want us experiencing the abundant life found in Christ. He wants us defeated, overwhelmed, beat down, depressed and full of doubt and unbelief. Satan sends his fiery darts and attacks every area of our lives. The reason he does this has to do with purpose … God's purpose.

The devil is after our *why* and our *what*. Satan's strategy is to keep our fruit trees barren and our lights turned off.

He wants us to walk away from good works, serving ourselves instead of God and others. He especially wants our children to follow that example. This is the very reason I put this chapter in this book.

The devil is a purpose thief.

Ephesians 6:11-12 "Put on the whole armor of God that you may be able to stand against the wiles of the devil. For we do not wrestle against flesh and blood, but against principalities, against powers, against the rulers of the darkness of this age, against spiritual hosts of wickedness in the heavenly places." NKJV

Think about what that scripture is saying. Here we are in this wresting match against what appears to be overwhelming odds. The very reason we are wrestling has to do with our purpose. Do you think the devil doesn't have a goal in mind, something he wants to achieve? Does he attack us just because he's mean, nasty, ugly and that's his job? What was his goal when he attacked Peter?

Luke 22:31-32 "And the Lord said, 'Simon, Simon! Indeed, Satan has asked for you, that he may sift you as wheat. But I have prayed for you, that your faith should not fail; and when you have returned to Me, strengthen your brethren.'" NKJV

Peter went through an intense wrestling match. Satan shot fiery darts of fear, doubt, and unbelief. Satan filled Peter's mind with these things, just like he does to us. In Peter's case, Satan is winning the match to the point Peter denies even knowing Jesus. But what was Satan's ultimate goal? It was God's purpose for Peter's life. Peter was the one taking the gospel to the Jews, and he was the one on whom Jesus would build His church. He was the one that had the revelation on the rooftop that God would extend His grace to the Gentiles, you and me.

The attacks coming on Peter's life were from the demonic realm. These attacks were far more about God's purpose for his life than just getting him down, depressed, and fearful. Similarly, the attacks on our life are far more about God's purposes for our life than just to get us down and depressed, full of fear and doubt.

I love what Jesus said to him in Luke 22:32, "But I have prayed for you that your faith should not fail." I believe that during every attack we go through and every wrestling match we have, our Lord and Savior is making intercession for us. Jesus is sitting at the right hand of the Father, interceding for His saints. Be aware when being attacked by the purpose thief - the devil and all those demonic forces you wrestle with – it's about robbing us of God's purpose. It's not about what seems obvious.

We may think that the devil wants us and our spouse arguing all the time to destroy our marriage. No, the devil wants to rob us of God's purpose. When we come under attack in any area of our life, understand what it's really about. It's about the very purpose for which God created, called, and chose us. The devil is a purpose thief.

If we have been losing those wrestling matches, I encourage that we stop wrestling naked. Historically, the wrestling matches he was referring to related to the ancient Greeks wrestling to the death, and they wrestled naked. If we are losing the wrestling matches with the demonic forces that are out to rob us of God's purpose, realize that the devil wants to kill us. Stop wrestling naked and put on the whole armor of God.

As written in *The Chronicles of Leroy*, "Naked devils are no match for those wearing God's armor."

Ephesians 6:13-18 "Therefore take up the whole armor of God that you may be able to withstand in the evil day, and having done all, to stand. Stand therefore, having girded your waist with truth, having put on the breastplate of righteousness. And having shod your feet with the preparation of the gospel of peace. Above all, taking the shield of faith with which you will be able to quench all the fiery darts of the wicked one. And take the helmet of salvation, and the sword of the Spirit, which is the Word of God. Praying always with all prayer and supplication in the Spirit, being watchful to this end with all perseverance and supplication for all the saints." NKJV

By the way, if we are not praying in the Spirit, we have a chink in our armor. Our challenge is to stop wrestling naked.

No doubt we have heard this message before and probably have even preached it. I want us to understand that there are many pastors and ministry leaders who really need to hear this. Maybe you're one of them because you have been suffering defeat after defeat, perhaps to the point you feel like giving up and giving in. The attack has been hard and heavy and you're losing the match.

I have a word from the Holy Spirit, stop wrestling

naked. Get up every morning, put on the armor of God and watch how quickly we begin to defeat our enemy. The devil is a purpose thief and that's why he goes about as a roaring lion, seeking whom he may devour. I don't believe he can devour our spirit when our spirit is born again. But I do believe he can devour your mind, will, and emotions. If he does that, he robs us of our purpose.

The next time you come under attack, feel depressed or overwhelmed by life, feel robbed of joy and peace, or find your sense of self-worth threatened, do the opposite of what you'd normally do. People have different ways of coping with depression, fear, doubt, and unbelief. If you normally crawl up in a ball feeling sorry for yourself, or go into hiding and become a recluse or maybe you indulge in some sort of destructive pattern or abuse, do the exact opposite of what you'd normally do when the enemy attacks. When that wrestling match starts, shine your light by loving someone, being kind, and bearing the fruit of the Spirit. Serve somewhere or someone, do a good deed or help somebody in need. If you have children, take them along.

This is how we defeat the enemy of our soul and rob him of his agenda. This is how we win the wrestling match. We don't win by surviving; we win by defeating. We win by pinning his neck down with our foot, putting the devil underfoot. Just surviving is a draw. Too often we settle for a draw and say to ourselves that I made it through that attack. Praise the Lord, I survived it.

Stop listening to the lion's roar. The devil goes about as a roaring lion seeking whom he may devour. Just like the lions in the jungles, they roar to establish fear and dominance. We must not allow them to establish fear and dominance in our lives. We must not listen to the lion's roar. That lion has no teeth. All that the devil has is a water pistol at best; spewing something that really can't hurt us. It just annoys us. We will start defeating this purpose thief when we realize he has no weapon formed against us that will prosper, we can protect our purpose.

Isaiah 54:17 "No weapon formed against you shall prosper; and every tongue which rises against you in judgment you shall condemn. This is the heritage of the servants of the Lord, and their righteousness is from Me, says the Lord." NKJV

Have you ever been held at gunpoint by a thief? I would imagine that would be a terrifying ordeal. I know if I were being held up at gunpoint, I would give the thief everything he wanted. But what if that thief was trying to rob you with what was obviously a water pistol, a kid's toy? Would you give him everything he wanted?

Can you imagine that scenario? The devil says, "Stick'em up and give me all your peace. Give me all your joy, your self-worth, and I'll take that fruit you're hiding from me. I'll also take that old flashlight that's barely shining."

Would we give him everything he wanted, especially when we're wielding a double-edged sword, the powerful word of God? No, we would not. Why? Because there are no teeth in that lion's mouth! He has no weapon that he can form against us that will prosper unless we let it.

We have absolute authority through the blood and name of Jesus to defeat the enemies of our soul. We don't have to give him what he's after. Use our authority, do the opposite of what we would normally do, and stop wrestling naked.

The second purpose thief is our flesh, that old carnal nature. In other words, my enemy is me. The one who keeps my light turned off, my fruit tree barren, my service record blank and my steps missing in my walk towards good work is me. As ministers, we all know we war against our flesh, but I wonder if we all have a complete understanding of why. It's all about our purpose.

Galatians 5:16 &17 "I say then: Walk in the Spirit, and you shall not fulfill the lust of the flesh. For the flesh lusts against the Spirit, and the Spirit against the flesh; and these contrary to one another, so that you do not do the things that you wish." NKJV

The flesh is referring to our old carnal nature. The part of us that desires to sin. This is that part of us that wants to rebel against God's will and disobey His word. The flesh controls us when we are not walking by the Spirit. Our flesh is a purpose thief. Purpose flows out of the Spirit and the flesh lusts and wars against our spirit (or conflicts with it). The word *lust* means to set the heart upon.

As one theologian put it, "The inclinations and desires of the flesh are contrary to those of the Spirit. They draw us away in an opposite direction, and while the Spirit of God would lead us one way, our carnal nature would lead us another. This produces the painful controversy which exists in our minds. The word *Spirit* here refers to the Spirit of God and to His influences on the heart."

Flesh is our purpose thief because purpose flows out of the Spirit. It's the Spirit who guides our steps toward good works. It's the Holy Spirit who enables us to bear the fruit of the Spirit. It's the Spirit within us that is the light we turn on in a world of darkness. It is the Spirit within us that ignites desires to serve and be the ministers God has called us to be.

Flesh is a purpose thief because purpose flows out of the Spirit. It is the Holy Spirit that gives us purpose and meaning for life. So, our great challenge is to walk in the Spirit, and not fulfill the lust of the flesh. That is what this race is all about, walking in the Spirit. So then, how do we do that? Some of us have heard this teaching for years, message after message that we are to walk in the Spirit and not fulfill the lust of the flesh. Yet often we are losing that battle. We find ourselves controlled by our flesh and robbed of God's purposes. Have you ever struggled with the dos and don'ts? Let's be honest with the Holy Spirit, we have all struggled with the dos and don'ts. Well, we're in good company.

The apostle Paul said in Romans 7:19 "I want to do what is good, but I don't. I don't want to do what is wrong, but I do it anyway." NLT

Then what is our answer to this purpose thief we call our flesh? How do we do the dos? How do we not do the don'ts? How do we walk in the Spirit and not fulfill the lust of the flesh?

I discovered my answer to this on the back roads of Ireland. During my sabbatical, my wife and I took a bucket list vacation to Ireland, Scotland, and England. We drove 4000 km driving on the back roads of these three countries. We looked at the castles, museums and towns, driving nearly 2500 miles. We stayed at a beautiful condominium and at different bed and breakfasts along the way.

In Scotland and Ireland, they don't have overpasses, they have roundabouts. If we're going north and want to go south, east or west, we must get on the roundabout. A roundabout is a big circle with multiple exits. Sometimes there are as many as six exits. We're traveling down the road with many roundabouts ahead. In fact, our GPS will tell us there is a roundabout coming up. Our GPS will locate us and let us know there is a roundabout in one mile or quarter mile. "Roundabout 500 meters, roundabout 100 meters." Our GPS is constantly preparing us for the roundabout and instructs us which exit to take on the roundabout. Each of the numerous exits will take us in a different direction.

So, here we go, about to get on the roundabout. We are to take the first exit and cars are spinning around the roundabout 50-60 miles an hour. We had to jump onto the roundabout weaving in and out of traffic, trying not to miss our correct exit. The entire time I'm driving with the steering wheel on the opposite side of the car, so I'm trying to drive the car, hit the brakes, hit the gas, and turn at our exit. I'm thinking we just must make it to the right exit and get off this roundabout, knowing if I miss the right exit, I have to keep going on the roundabout or take the wrong exit. We kept going round and round, with the GPS sounding in my ear.

This is the point of the story; we have to choose the right exit on the roundabout. We must listen to the Holy Spirit and choose the correct exit on the roundabout. It's all about our choice on the roundabout, gassing when we need to give it gas, braking when we need to hit the brakes, and getting off at the right time. If we missed it, as we so often do, we just stay on the roundabout until our exit comes up again. See, we choose to walk in the Spirit. We choose our dos and our don'ts. It's a choice we make when we see the roundabout coming up. It's a choice we make when we hear the Holy Spirit locate us and He says "Roundabout coming up! Take the right exit." This is how we defeat the purpose thief that we call the flesh.

This is a good place for the Holy Spirit to ask, "Are you on the roundabout? What exit do you need to take so that you will not be robbed of your purpose?" The problem is my flesh and if my flesh is crucified, sin has nothing to eat. Sin cannot feed on dead, crucified flesh.

Galatians 2:20 "I have been crucified with Christ; it is no longer I who live, but Christ lives in me; and the life which I now live in the flesh, I live by faith in the Son of God, who loved me and gave Himself for me." NKJV

The problem is not sin. The problem is live flesh. How do we get victory over the flesh? We crucify the flesh, put to death our old carnal nature, and walk by faith. As Leroy says, "Moral decisions lead to divine destinations, immoral decisions lead to demonic devastation."

This makes repentance our pathway to victory. But how do we walk by the Spirit? We walk by the Spirit by being dependent on the Spirit. This makes repentance and dependence our pathway to victory. Dependency is defined by Webster as "to hang on, to be sustained by being fastened or attached to something above." This word is defined as to *rely on*. To have such a connection with anything that, without it, the effect would not be produced. It means to rest with confidence, to trust, to have full confidence or belief.

Do we depend on the Holy Spirit? Are we dependent upon the Holy Spirit as we think about those besetting sins operating in our life? Is there dependence on God concerning those habitual sins that have such power in our life, because of our flesh? Are we holding onto the Lord, resting with our confidence in Him? Are we being sustained because we are attached firmly to the Lord? Dependence is our pathway to victory over our flesh.

Proverbs 3:5 "Trust in the Lord with all your heart; do not depend on your own understanding." NLT

Too often we are only dependent on God when we have to be. When we are in that situation where there is no other way out, when everything else has failed, and our world comes crashing down and our troubles are overwhelming. Then, we find ourselves depending on God, trusting God, and resting in Him.

What would it be like if we were dependent upon the Lord one hundred percent of the time? Not fifty percent of the time. Not twenty percent of the time, but one hundred percent of the time? Do we think our lives would look like the victorious Christian life that Jesus came to give us? Do we think it would look like victory over flesh?

I have found that flesh can't control me when I'm one hundred percent dependent upon the Lord. When I am one hundred percent trusting in Him, resting in Him, and hanging on to Him, I have victory over flesh when I am attached to Him firmly, no longer can doubt, unbelief, fear, or confusion control me. Our pathway to victory is dependence. It is our dependence on His righteousness, not our own, our dependence on His power, not our own willpower. Everything we need to live in victory has been given to us.

Galatians 5:16 "I say then: Walk in the Spirit, and you shall not fulfill the lust of the flesh." NKJV

To walk in the Spirit is to make one's way, to progress, to make use of opportunities, to regulate one's life.

Galatians 5:16 "So I say, let the Holy Spirit guide your lives. Then you won't be doing what your sinful nature craves." NLT

A commentary on this says, "Walk by the Spirit, according to the rule and direction of the Holy Spirit, who is the higher conscience and controlling principle of the Christian."

Galatians 4:6 "And because we are His children, God

has sent the Spirit of His Son into our hearts, prompting us to call out, 'Abba, Father'." NLT

Romans 8:2 "And because you belong to Him, the power of the life-giving spirit has freed you from the power of sin that leads to death." NLT

So let us a draw a conclusion together. I know my problem is my flesh. I know my answer is being Spirit controlled. I know I have everything I need for victory. I have righteousness and grace that gives me strength and power. So, righteousness, strength, and power have been given to us. My righteousness comes through Jesus.

Romans 5:19 "For as by one man's disobedience many were made sinners, so also by one man's obedience many will be made righteous." NKJV

My strength comes through God's grace.

2 Corinthians 12:9 "And He said to me, 'My grace is sufficient for you, for My strength is made perfect in weakness.' Therefore, most gladly I will rather boast in my infirmities, that the power of Christ may rest upon me." NKJV

My power comes through the Holy Spirit.

ACTS 1:8 "But you shall receive power when the Holy Spirit has come upon you; and you shall be witnesses to me in Jerusalem, and in all Judea and Samaria, and to the end of the earth." NKJV

Everything we need to live in victory has been given to us: righteousness, strength, and power. Do you believe this?

Then why does the flesh still hold on to us? How it is that habitual sin still controls our lives when we have all we need to live the victorious Christian life, when we have everything we need to be over comers, when we have this position of righteousness or right standing with God? If we have the power of the Holy Spirit in us, why do those besetting sins still have power in our lives?

It is because of independence. If we are independent of the Holy Spirit, instead of dependent on the Holy Spirit, it is because our dependence is less than one hundred percent. We can be dependent upon God's righteousness, and not our own. We can trust in God's grace that is sufficient when we are weak, but if we are living independent of the Holy Spirit's power operating in our life, we find ourselves defeated by our besetting sins. So, our victory is our dependence on the Holy Spirit dwelling in us.

How do we live in victory over our flesh? It is our dependence. If we are not living in victory over our flesh, we have to ask ourselves where are we going wrong. If we're still struggling on the roundabout, where are we going wrong? First off, we go wrong when we focus on the sin, rather than on the Spirit. Our focus is on that repulsive, ugly, sinful thing we are saying or doing, rather than on our dependence on the Holy Spirit. Our focus is on the sin, rather than our dependence on the Holy Spirit.

I'm reminded of how a dog trainer trains a puppy to stop his destructive behavior, such as chewing on things he shouldn't be chewing on. The trainer trains the puppy to keep his eyes on his master, not on what has the puppy's attention. Likewise, we are to keep our eyes on the Master, not on those destructive things we give our attention to.

Another place we go wrong is that we place value on something that has no value. The desires of our flesh and our besetting sins add absolutely no value to our life. We may think it does. The devil tries to convince us it does, but the truth is they have no value. They only bring sorrow, regret, guilt and shame. We often place significance on things that have no value at all. It's like the pet rocks of the 1970s. Gary Dahl came up with a marketing scheme to sell people pet rocks. He sold the pet rocks for $3.95 each. If we would send him the money, he would send us a pet rock. His claims were that this pet rock would comfort us, make us happy, and would not cost us anything to keep it and maintain it. We could get all of this for only $3.95. It's reported that he sold 1.5 million pet rocks in six months and made $5.9 million dollars. People bought into his idea and placed value on a rock that had no ability to bring comfort or happiness, it had no value. They could have gone out into a gravel parking lot and picked up their own pet rock.

When it comes to our sinful flesh, the devil is trying to sell us a pet rock. Our flesh has no value in our life. It does not comfort us. It does not make us happy. And it costs a fortune to maintain. So, where we go wrong is thinking that our besetting sin or other desires of our flesh adds some kind of value to us, and it doesn't. It only brings sorrow, regret, shame, and guilt. Another place where we go wrong is when we don't understand God's purpose in our struggles.

1 Peter 1:15-16 "But as He who called you is holy: you also be holy in all your conduct. Because it is written, 'Be holy, for I am holy'." NKJV

Holiness is only proven when tested, just as faith and obedience are proven when tested. Besetting sins will test our walk of holiness before the Lord.

After the children of Israel came into the Promised Land, the Lord left enemies in the land in order to teach the next generation how to fight. Our struggles can teach us how to do spiritual warfare. Often deliverance is just on the other side of the fight. So those besetting sins can teach us how to do spiritual warfare and they can test our commitment to holiness. Most importantly, God's purpose in those struggles teaches us how to be dependent on the Holy Spirit. God's desire is for us to live in victory over besetting sins, but that victory comes through dependence, and that dependence is tested by those struggles.

God's purpose is dependence, and dependence is only proven when tested. We have to ask ourselves when we don't live in victory, even though we have taken the pathway of deliverance and repentance, what is God's purpose for the struggles we are having with our besetting sins? What is God working on in us through the struggles? For many Christians He's opening their eyes to their need for repentance, for others it's a need for deliverance, and for some, if not all, their need for dependence.

I want to say something as I finish up this chapter that may surprise you. Stop striving. Please stop striving! As we struggle for victory over our besetting sins, or any area of our flesh where we just cannot find victory, stop striving. I'm not saying to stop fighting; I'm saying to stop striving. Our victory is in our dependence on the Lord. We need total dependence on His righteousness, His grace that is sufficient for our weaknesses and His power that comes through the Holy Spirit in us. Our striving comes through our independence. Our striving comes as we labor to become righteous in our self-efforts. Our striving comes when we try to overcome in our own strength.

It is when we stop striving and become totally dependent upon the Holy Spirit that we can defeat the purpose thieves and experience the success that comes from the title of purpose driven.

FOUR

THEY CALL ME A STRATEGIST
NAVIGATING THROUGH THE SCHEMES AND TACTICS OF YOUR ADVERSARY

Pastor or ministry leader, it is because our adversary, the devil, is a strategist that we must become strategists. Satan has many schemes to destroy us, our families, our ministries, our health, and our churches. I pray we don't take this task lightly.

Ephesians 6:12 "For we are not fighting against flesh and blood enemies, but against evil rulers and authorities of the unseen world, against mighty powers in this dark world, and against evil spirits in the heavenly places." NLT

2 Corinthians 2:11 "So that Satan will not outsmart us. For we are familiar with his evil schemes."

We must become strategists. Our fight is both offensive and defensive. Many leaders only fight a defensive fight. When the attack comes upon their lives or ministries, only then do they engage in spiritual warfare. Only then do they put together a strategy for victory over the enemy. Our challenge is to become offensive in our fight, not just defensive. We must put a plan in place that keeps us alert to the schemes of the enemy and ready to do spiritual warfare when necessary. We won't win those spiritual battles that are coming against our church or ministry by ourselves. It takes a team. Our greatest asset when the assault comes is an intercessory prayer team that will engage in spiritual warfare on our behalf, and on the behalf of our ministry.

YOUR STRATEGY BEGINS WITH AN INTERCESSORY PRAYER TEAM

Intercessors are called prayer warriors for a reason. They are like soldiers on the front lines. They are the Special Forces in God's army. Intercessors are those who have been called by the Lord to pray and intercede for us, our family, our ministry, our staff and the church. Intercessors are those who are mature enough to engage the enemy on his turf. Intercessors are those who are loyal to you and who you trust enough to confide in. Make sure they have an armor bearer mentality. There is a must-read book titled *God's Armor Bearer* by Terry Nance. I recommend this book to intercessors, staff or people you are building on. This can be a game changer for your ministry and the health of your church, your family, and your personal life.

Pastors, we must find these intercessors in our churches or among those involved in our ministries and form a team. Then place your personal intercessor in a position of leadership over that team. That personal intercessor must be someone you can trust to share things that are confidential and who is able to communicate to the team in a proper way, so they don't uncover you or anyone else. This is one of the strategies against our adversary, the devil.

We look for these people among those who have a passion for prayer and seeking the Lord. These are the ones who show up to the prayer meetings at the church. These are the ones that we know for a fact are people of prayer and faith.

King David was a strategist. Each time he went to war against his enemy, he first sought the Lord for counsel.

2 Samuel 5:22 -25 "Then the Philistines went up once again and deployed themselves in the Valley of Rephaim. Therefore, David inquired of the Lord, and He said, 'You shall not go up; circle around behind them, and come upon them in front of the mulberry trees. And it shall be, when you hear the sound of marching in the tops of the mulberry trees, they you shall advance quickly. For then the Lord will go out before you to strike the camp of the Philistines.' And David did so, as the Lord commanded him; and he drove back the Philistines from Geba as far as Gezer." NKJV

The Lord gave King David a strategy for victory, and He will do the same for us. Each strategy for warfare begins with seeking the Lord. Each strategy for accomplishing what God has called us to do begins with seeking the Lord. Don't assume yesterday's strategy for victory is today's strategy or for the next thing God puts on our heart to accomplish.

2 Chronicles 26:3-5 "Uzziah was sixteen years old when he became king, and he reigned in Jerusalem 52 years. His mother was Jecoliah from Jerusalem. He did what was

pleasing in the Lord's sight, just as his father, Amaziah, had done. And as long as the king sought guidance from the Lord, God gave him success." NLT

As long as the king sought guidance from the Lord, God gave him success. New destinations require new strategies from the Lord. Someone said that good is the enemy of the best! Therefore, a good strategy is the enemy of the best strategy. It's good to listen to people, but it's best to listen to God. When the Lord's strategy is made known to us, that's when we engage our special forces, our intercessors. Communicate well with your intercessory prayer team the needs and concerns you have, as well as what the Lord has put on your heart to accomplish. Your strategy is to engage them in the battle, the battle that rages over your goals and your vision. You will discover that you can break the back of the enemy through intercession.

Another strategy is corporate prayer.

Matthew 16:19 "And I will give you the keys of the kingdom of heaven, and whatever you bind on earth with be bound in heaven, and whatever you loose on earth will be loosed in heaven." NKJV

Something powerful happens when the church prays. Give the strategy to the intercessory prayer team and those in the church body who will pray. Remember, our goal is to become a strategist because our adversary is a strategist. Develop strategies for when the church or ministry comes under attack. Develop strategies for your vision and your goals. Develop a strategy when you come under attack personally, whether that comes in the form of people coming against you or the temptation to sin.

Lay hold of what is written in *The Chronicles of Leroy*. "The devil knows your favorite candy!" The devil knows the sin that is our greatest temptation. Never forget the devil will scheme a whole year to cause us to fall in one night. The demonic realm knows which strategies will result in a stumble or fall. Pastors and ministry leaders must have a strategy to defeat the schemes of the devil and his demonic realm.

In my experience there are five temptations every minister can be tempted by. I use the words "can be" because it doesn't mean every minister yields to these temptations it just means that these temptations are strategies of the demonic realm to rob us of God's calling in our lives. We have seen great men and women fall to one or more of these temptations and it breaks our heart, and no doubt grieves the Holy Spirit.

In *The Chronicles of Leroy*, they are called the five temptations for every minister which are Glory, Gold, Girls, Guys and Gluttony.

The temptation of Glory is the temptation to take unto ourselves that which belongs to the Lord, His glory. This temptation allows people to set us up on a pedestal that belongs to God alone. This can happen because of all that God is doing through us and the work of the ministry.

People set us on a pedestal because of how God is using us. The glory is a great temptation for many leaders and it's easy to yield to this temptation without even realizing it.

We naturally want affirmation from people because it brings encouragement to us. Encouragement is always good and needed in the work of the ministry. However, when we have to have that affirmation in order to feel secure or for whatever reason we feel we need to be elevated in people's eyes it becomes a problem, and the temptation is from Satan. I will tell you without a doubt, God will knock us off that pedestal just so the people who put us on it can watch us fall. All glory belongs to the Lord.

1Timothy 1:17 "All honor and glory to God forever and ever! He is the eternal king, the unseen one who never dies; he alone is God. Amen." NLT

Think about what drove Satan. What ended up causing him to be cast out of heaven? He wanted what was to be given to God alone, the glory.

There are only two directions to go when the Lord uses us in a mighty way and people begin to put us on a pedestal. We either let them do it and allow that pride to set us on a course of destruction, or we refuse to let them and allow humility to govern our words and actions encouraging them to give all glory unto the Lord.

James 4:6 "But He gives more grace. Therefore, He says: 'God resists the proud, but gives grace to the humble'." NKJV

There are only two directions: pride or humility. One direction God resists the other direction He embraces. Which direction will you choose?

The Gold, I am speaking here of the temptation of money. The devil tempts ministers to the point that the ministry becomes about money. The motivation for doing all God has called you to do, is tainted by the love of money. We have all seen ministers and ministries that started out pure, but the gold became the great temptation that led them to their downfall.

1 Timothy 6:10 "For the love of money is a root of all kinds of evil, for which some have strayed from the faith in their greediness and pierced themselves through with many sorrows." NKJV

We are to be stewards, not owners. It's wise to keep what belongs to God in His hands. If the gold is in His hands, He can do great and mighty things. The best way for us to keep it in the Lord's hands is through accountability. If there is no accountability in the finances of the ministry, we can become a target for accusation. It doesn't matter whether we're guilty or not, because with accusation, comes the appearance of guilt. In the world we are innocent until proven guilty. But sadly, too often in the church, we are guilty until proven innocent. Even then, a stigma of guilt remains throughout the life of the ministry.

We must have a team of people who are accountable for the finances of our church or ministry. We must put the gold in their hands. This way, we avoid even the appearance of evil. This team of people should be in submission to our counsel and vision concerning those finances, and as leaders we should be in submission to their counsel as well.

Let me ask you a question, who has hold of the gold? Is it in your hands, or the Lord's?

The next temptation involves Girls. It's the girls that

play with the lust of man's flesh. How many stories have we heard of men or women of God involved in promiscuity and sexual immorality? How many stories have we heard of these men and women falling to the temptation to commit adultery? How many leaders have left their spouses and the work of the ministry due to the temptation of the flesh? How many ministers today, in active ministry, struggle with pornography? It is written in *The Chronicles of Leroy*: "A girl is often the favorite candy Satan sells to those willing to pay the price." I will add it's a high price to pay.

The crucified life is the answer to the lust that would drive us to bad destinations. The best advice I can offer is if you find yourself lusting after another person or anything, tell on the devil. Let me say that a little louder. Tell on the devil!

Tell on the devil when temptation comes. Tell your spouse who is your first line of defense. Confess to them what's going on in your mind and your heart. Tell your pastor. Tell your armor bearers who you know have your back. If you don't have a pastor or armor bearer, I suggest you get them because you will need them.

We must remember, it's not just about us. It's about the next generation. It's about our sons and daughters, and the calling of God on their lives. It's about the next generation that is being raised up in the church. It's about the ministry and the impact that the ministry loses when we fall. We must remember, it's not just about us or our lust. It's about the demonic attack on our marriage and our ministry. We must realize there is a scheme of the enemy, and he will scheme an entire year to cause us to fall in one night.

So, tell on the devil. Tell your spouse, pastor and armor bearers you are accountable to. Recognize the scheme for what it is and tell on the devil. Don't let your pride guarantee your defeat.

In *The Chronicles of Leroy*, it says, "Moral decisions lead to divine destinations, immoral decisions lead to demonic devastation."

Now let's move on to Guys. I will define this as the temptation of the fear of man.

This temptation could come in the form of homosexuality, which we have seen many great men and women of God fall to. But what I'm primarily speaking about is the fear of man, the temptation to let the fear of man control you.

Will you become a hireling or a shepherd? This is the fear of what they can do to hinder our ministry. It's also the fear of what they won't do to support our ministry. Fear will drive us to become a hireling instead of the shepherd God has called us to be. The devil finds more success in our church if we are a hireling than he does by us leaving that church because we refuse to be a hireling.

John 10:10-13 "The thief does not come except to steal and to kill and to destroy. I have come that they may have life, and that they may have it more abundantly. I am the good Shepherd. The good shepherd GIVES His life for the sheep. But a hireling, he who is not the shepherd, one who does not own the sheep, sees the wolf coming and leaves the sheep and flees; and the wolf catches the sheep and scatters them. The hireling flees because he is a hireling and does not care about the sheep." NKJV

The fear of man has been the downfall of countless ministers and has robbed the world of the vision God placed upon their hearts. In my experience, pastors and ministry leaders desperately want to take their ministry to God's destinations, but the fear of man won't let them. God's control, not man's control, is our only hope for our future. It requires faith, trust, obedience, and courage to turn things around. We don't have to fear man, only God. It's a choice we make. It's a choice we have to live with.

Could it cost us our position, our livelihood? Yes, depending on how the government and bylaws of our church are set up. I'll speak more about that in another chapter or perhaps another book. So yes, it could cost us everything. That's the price tag on refusing to be a hireling. Would we rather stand before God and give an account of being a good shepherd or a hireling, someone who fears God or fears man?

It's faith, trust, obedience, and courage that overcomes the fear of man. Three separate times the Lord told Joshua to have courage. It's interesting that the Lord repeated Himself three times. No doubt having courage is something we need to be reminded of often as we face the challenges of ministry and the confrontations of man.

God put authorities in our lives to guard us, help us and give us wise counsel. Godly authorities are truly a blessing. However, Satan will put people in our way to try to control us, our church, and ministry, thereby hindering God's purpose and vision so we must discern between the two.

Glory, Gold, Girls, Guys, and lastly Gluttony.

I am speaking about the great temptation to overindulge in some form. It's basically indulging in anything that is harmful to your health. I am not speaking about being overweight but the overindulgence of any kind, which could include food, alcohol, prescription medications, overspending, gambling, soft drinks, etc, you get the idea.

The devil's strategy is threefold. First, it's for them to have poor health and second is to be a bad example for others to follow. Thirdly, it's to rob them of God's calling and purpose through premature death. The challenge is to be mindful of what we put into our bodies, stay fit and avoid any other overindulgence in order to lead by example and fulfill God's purpose.

Philippians 3:14-16 "I press toward the goal for the prize of the upward call of God in Christ Jesus. Therefore, let us, as many as are mature, have this mind; and if in anything you think otherwise, God will reveal even this to you. Nevertheless, to the degree that we have already attained, let us walk by the same rule, let us be of the same mind." NKJV

It's so important to avoid this temptation. We know gluttony and the poor health that accompanies it have sent many ministers to a premature death.

Numbers 11:34 "So that place was called Kibroth-Hattaavah (which means "graves of gluttony") because there they buried the people who had craved meat from Egypt." NLT

Ezekiel 16:49 "Sodom's sins were pride, gluttony, and laziness, while the poor and needy suffered outside her door." NLT

1 Corinthians 6:12-13 "All things are lawful for me, but all things are not helpful. All things are lawful for me, but I will not be brought under the power of any. Foods for the stomach and stomach for the foods, but God will destroy both it and them. Now the body is not for sexual immorality but for the Lord, and the Lord for the body." NKJV

Is it hard for us to get bad eating habits or any type of overindulgence under control? Will it take effort? Yes, but isn't the longevity of our ministry worth it? Will our eternal reward in heaven not be greater because of the longevity of our ministry? Yes.

Again, the devil knows your favorite candy and he will scheme to tempt you to taste it and keep tasting it. Glory, gold, girls, guys, and gluttony are the five things Satan tempts every minister of God with.

Does the devil know your favorite candy? If it is glory, repent and keep God receiving all that belongs to Him. If it is gold, repent and keep your motivations pure and stay accountable. If it's girls, repent and tell on the devil. If it's guys, repent and have courage and determination to fear God alone. If it's gluttony, repent and live daily the crucified life, putting the longevity of your ministry above the satisfaction of your flesh.

No doubt there are far more than these five temptations that Satan uses to tempt us so feel free to add to the list whatever the Lord is speaking to you about. However, knowing the strategy for victory is the same, repentance, faith, trust, obedience, courage and living the crucified life. This strategy will lead us to victory so that we may be called by God, the church, our peers and the demonic realm a strategist.

FIVE

THEY CALL ME A LOVER

NAVIGATING THROUGH THE CHALLENGES OF MAINTAINING A CULTURE OF LOVE AND HONOR

One of the greatest challenges we face in our churches, or the development of our ministries, is establishing a culture of love and honor. Peter Drucker, a legendary business management consultant and writer, says that culture eats strategy for breakfast. We can have a great strategy for accomplishing our mission and vision, but the wrong culture will destroy it.

My son, Justin Coffman who serves as the executive pastor of our church and as the current mayor of Midlothian, says you must define your culture because it will ultimately define you. I will add that culture is only proven when tested. It is when problems arise in the church that we find what kind of culture we have. Is it a culture of love and honor, or is it a culture of criticism, backbiting, murmuring, and gossip? Will your people support you, or will they form a coup? As one of my former worship pastors, Levi Corrao once said, "Culture is always tested in the fire."

I want to recommend some books to you from those who can say it so much better than I can. Then I'll give my opinion as someone who I hope is called a lover.

A Culture of Honor by Danny Silk and Bill Johnson.

The Advantage and The Five Dysfunctions of a Team by Patrick Lencioni.

Experience has proven that culture is established by the leadership team, beginning with the senior pastor or ministry leader. When we honor those in our care, they will honor us. If we show love to those in our care, they will show love to us and from there, it all trickles down. We love and honor our staff members, volunteers, church members, whether they are serving or not, supporting or not. We just love them.

Let them hear words of appreciation, encouragement, adoration, and affirmation. Let them see your love manifesting for them. Let others see you honoring them because love and honor looks and sounds like something. Just as dishonor looks like something and sounds like something. Perhaps you have heard the sound of it.

1 Corinthians 13 is worthy of an in-depth study and goes to great lengths to tell us what love looks like and sounds like. Sadly, many churches show little, if any, honor to their pastor producing all kinds of problems in their church, whether they see it or not.

Romans 12:10 "Love each other with genuine affection and take delight in honoring each other." NLT

1 Corinthians 12:23-25 "And those members of the body which we think to be less honorable, on these we bestow greater honor; and our unpresentable parts have greater modesty, but our presentable parts have no need. But God composed the body, having given greater honor to that part which lacks it, that there should be no schism in the body, but that the members should have the same care for one another." NKJV

1 Timothy 5:17 "Let the elders who rule well be counted worthy of double honor, especially those who labor in the word and doctrine." NKJV

I started to title this chapter *Culture Wars* because we have to navigate through the fires of church culture. Take a moment to read Ed Herald's story in Chapter 12. Ed tells the story of how the culture of a church can burn the church to the ground.

One of the greatest ongoing challenges we face in ministry, is maintaining the culture of Christ in our church or ministry. One way culture is defined in the dictionary is the "attitude and behavioral characteristics of a particular social group". Therefore, we could define a Christ-like culture in our church or ministry team as having the attitude and the behavioral characteristics of Jesus.

Though I've not found a scripture that specifically uses the word culture as it relates to the culture of Christ or church culture, the scriptures do reveal the Christ-like character and attitude expected of both the early church and the current church. For example, Jesus said in John 13:34: "A new commandment I give to you, that you love one another; as I have loved you, that you also love one another." NKJV

"*As I have loved you*" gives us all the instructions we need.

Luke 22:26-27 "But among you it will be different. Those who are the greatest among you should take the lowest rank, and the leader should like a servant. Who is more important, the one who sits at the table or the one who serves? The one who sits at the table, of course. But not here! For I am among you as one who serves." NLT

Love, service, and sacrifice are our keys to developing a Christ-like culture.

The apostle Paul said in Philippians 2:1-7; "Therefore if there is any consolation in Christ, if any comfort of love, if any fellowship of the Spirit, if any affection and mercy, fulfill my joy by being like-minded, having the same love, being in one accord of one mind. Let nothing be done through selfish ambition or conceit, but in lowliness of mind let each esteem others better than himself. Let each of you look out not only for his own interests, but also for the interests of others. Let this mind be in you which was also in Christ Jesus. Who, being in the form of God, did not consider it robbery to be equal with God, but made Himself of no reputation, taking the form of a bondservant, and coming the likeness of men." NKJV

The apostle Paul, whose life reflected Christ, had the attitude and behavioral characteristics of Jesus. As

Christians, and especially as pastors and leaders, we recognize our need to reflect Christ-like attitudes and behavior. We could do studies on Christ-likeness and the importance of it in our church and personal lives. The problem comes when our culture goes through the fire and it is tested. It is tested by problems in the ministry, people who are offended, people who don't trust us, and people who want what they want in spite of us.

As pastors and ministry leaders we stand in the way of what people who disagree with us want. I'll speak more about that dilemma in a later chapter. But culture is tested and only proven when the fire comes. The overall attitude and character of a church or ministry team is revealed in how people respond or react when the fire comes and will either reveal Christ-likeness or something totally different. That is the culture war.

You have probably experienced a church or ministry meeting where there was accusation, anger, strife, jealousy, backbiting, slander, self-ambition and dishonoring of leadership. Basically, no one looked or acted like Jesus. You have probably been in meetings where the ugliness of the flesh and demonic control got the best of people. The problem is the culture. The problem is not the disagreements with decisions; nor is it the opinions. The problem is in the culture.

I once knew a very good man of God who held the position of a deacon. At one of the deacon meetings, he was struck in the head by another deacon out of anger. He was an older man and later suffered a premature death as a result of the altercation. This is alarming, very sad and shouldn't have ever happened. This church definitely had a culture problem.

James 3:13-18 "If you are wise and understand God's ways, prove it by living an honorable life, doing good works with the humility that comes from wisdom. But if you are bitterly jealous and there is selfish ambition in your heart, don't cover up the truth with boasting and lying. For jealousy and selfishness are not God's kind of wisdom. Such things are earthly, unspiritual, and demonic." NLT

Can you see the two cultures James is speaking about? Obviously, when the flesh wins the culture war, there is all matter of the demonic associated with it. So, how is the culture war won? How do we navigate through the fire? How do we establish a culture of love and honor? How is a Christ-like culture maintained in your church or ministry team? It begins with you, the leader.

There are many great teachings in scripture that reveal the Christ-like culture that should be established in the church that we can and should teach on.

Here are some examples:

A culture of love revealed. 1 Corinthians 13

A culture of morality revealed. 1 Corinthians 9-10

A culture of holiness revealed. 1 John

A culture of helping people revealed. 1 Corinthians 7

A culture of giving revealed. 1 Corinthians 16

A culture of honor is revealed in how the apostles were treated and how they treated others is presented throughout the New Testament. All these teachings will only win the culture war temporarily if we're not leading the way. We must lead the way by our Christ-like characteristics, actions and attitudes. We can teach and preach on having a Christ-like culture in the church, but if our philosophy of ministry is subject to worldly thinking, we lose the culture war.

Whether we realize it or not, we operate in our church or ministry with a philosophy of ministry. It's a way of thinking that governs how we're going to accomplish our ministry and whatever our philosophy is will affect the culture of our church either in a positive or negative way.

There are two basic philosophies of ministry that set the culture in a church or ministry. First is the philosophy of "mission over the man" and second is the philosophy of "man over the mission".

The philosophy of mission over the man is a philosophy that drives us as a leader to accomplish our mission and doing all God has put on our heart to do. It's a philosophy that drives us to accomplish the mission no matter what. After all, God has given us the mission and His instructions to accomplish it. Whether that looks like reaching the lost, sending people to the mission field, developing and educating leadership, building a building, discipleship, water baptisms, or developing future ministries, starting campus churches, or anything else. It's our mission, and it's the most important thing!

Although we wouldn't say it or even be willing to admit it, our mission is more important than anything else. Deep down inside, we know it drives us more than anything else or anyone else. And though we would never do it intentionally or with malice, the mission drives us, even to the point of hurting people if they stand in the way of the mission. This philosophy of mission over the man is in way too many churches and the result is wounded and defrauded Christian brothers and sisters all over the world. I've heard it said that the Christian army is the only army that shoots its wounded. This philosophy of ministry often proves that statement true. Do you know that mission over the man is a military philosophy?

As an Army Drill Instructor in the 70s during the Vietnam War, our job was to train the new recruits to follow orders. This process included drill and ceremony, marching, physical training and developing various combat skills all for the purpose of training them to follow orders and preparing them for battle. Training by the drill sergeant was necessary so that the soldiers could accomplish the mission no matter what the cost, even if it cost them their lives. It's mission over the man.

This philosophy is necessary in a military combat situation whether taking Hamburger Hill in Vietnam, or storming the beaches in Normandy during World War II. The goal to accomplish the mission no matter what the cost is a military philosophy.

Sadly, this same philosophy is the philosophy of many churches, pastors, and ministry leaders. This philosophy has cost many people in the body of Christ their emotional and mental well-being. In some cases, it cost them their spiritual lives. This ministry philosophy has left many wounded soldiers who are no longer engaged in service at the church. Some have even fallen from the faith because of it. It's a military philosophy that puts the importance of mission over the importance of people. It begins with leadership and trickles down, impacting the culture of the entire church or ministry team.

The second philosophy of ministry that will impact your culture is man over mission. This means that you are more important than what you do. It's a philosophy that establishes a culture of love and honor, regardless of whether people are serving or not. It's choosing the people over the mission, the vision, or even reaching your goals.

Did Jesus die for you or for what you could do for Him? Are you more important to Him because of who you are or for what you're doing? He did not die for you because of what you would do for Him. He died because of the great love He has for you.

We are more important to Him than what we do for Him. People should be more important to us than what they do for us. If we never did anything else for God in our life or ministry, He still loves us. He cares more about us than what we do. With that settled, if we reflect this to others it will transform the culture of our church or ministry and trickle down into our leadership, our teams, and the entire church.

What does this philosophy of ministry look like practically as we are trying to accomplish the mission? In addition to honoring one another with our words and actions and showing appreciation to everyone – whether they are serving or not – we should value every person in the church so they know they are truly appreciated. Equally important is loving people, which helps establish a strong, positive culture. This kind of love is what I like to call, *Loving People Past*.

I tell my staff and everyone who becomes a leader of ministry at Harvest Hill, if you are going to be in ministry with me you must love people, and this kind of love looks like something. It looks like loving people past.

First, it means we must love people past our personality differences. At times in church and in ministry, personalities can clash. People have different personalities than ours and often those differences can clash. People see things differently; opinions can vary according to the personality a person has and we must love them past those personality differences.

Secondly, we must love people past their character flaws. People have flaws in their character, and this can cause many issues to come up between us and them. People are not perfect, including you and me. We must love them past their character flaws. This does not mean we don't speak into their lives, addressing those character issues as the Holy Spirit directs. It just means we love them in spite of those flaws.

Thirdly, I tell people who would like to be in ministry with me, you have to love people past their sin issues. We all struggle with sin issues; those things that we know are missing God's mark. Those sin issues can look like the words people speak, the things they do, and even the attitudes they have. It is said that God only sent one totally sinless preacher, and it was certainly not me or you. His name is Jesus. So, we love people past their sin issues. Again, it doesn't mean we don't address those sin issues, we do, but we address those sin issues with love and honor with the goal being repentance.

Fourthly, we love people past their offenses. People will offend us with their words, attitudes, and actions. How we respond to them with the character and attitude we have will affect the Christ-like culture we want to establish.

Lastly, we have to love people past our rightness. By that I mean, loving them past when we know we are right concerning the situation or conflict. We know that we are right, and they are wrong. The temptation can be in our rightness that we forget to love. I'll say that a little louder. In our rightness, we forget to love. It's like when the Pharisees confronted Jesus about working on the Sabbath by healing people. In their perceived rightness, they forgot to love. Basically, what I tell people who want to serve with me in ministry is that you have to love people with a First Corinthians kind of love.

1 Corinthians 13:4-8 "Love suffers long and is kind; love does not envy; love does not parade itself, is not puffed up; does not behave rudely, does not seek its own, is not provoked, thinks no evil; bears all things, believes all things, hopes all things, endures all things. Love never fails." NKJV

To be in ministry with me, you must love people. Love

looks like something, acts like something, and sounds like something.

As is written in *The Chronicles of Leroy,* "Love is determined by the depth of your efforts, not the shallowness of your words."

1 Peter 4:8 "And above all things have fervent love for one another, for love will cover a multitude of sins." NKJV

This philosophy of ministry will establish a Christ-like culture in our churches and ministries. When we add to our philosophy of ministry loving people past, valuing people, encouraging people and showing appreciation to people, the cultural war is won. However, I'm not saying we should devalue our mission, vision, and purpose, nor should we, in any way, shape or form devalue our goals for fulfilling them. The Lord's desire is that we accomplish what He's called us to accomplish.

We are to be about our Father's business and setting goals, accomplishing our mission and fulfilling our vision which are all of excellent value in God's eyes. All I'm saying as important as these things are, the people God has placed into your care are more important. This philosophy of ministry is man over the mission.

Now before I finish up this chapter, there are situations where the man becomes the mission. It's in these situations that we have to confront the man or woman for the sake of God's vision for their lives, and our vision as well.

A good example of this is when Moses' sister, Miriam, was struck with leprosy after criticizing Moses. It says the whole camp was held up. Obviously, Moses chose man over the mission, but at the same time she became the mission.

Numbers 12:9-16 "So the anger of the Lord was aroused against them, and He departed. And when the cloud departed from above the tabernacle, suddenly Miriam became leprous, as white as snow. Then Aaron turned toward Miriam, and there she was, a leper. So, Aaron said to Moses, 'Oh, my Lord! Please do not lay this sin on us, in which we have done foolishly and in which we have sinned. Please do not let her be as one dead, whose flesh is half consumed when he come out of his mother's womb!' So, Moses cried out to the Lord, saying, 'Please heal her, O God, I pray!' Then the Lord said to Moses, 'If her father had put spit in her face, would she not be shamed seven days? Let her be shut out of the camp seven days, and afterward she may be received again.' So, Miriam was shut out of the camp seven days and the people did not journey till Miriam was brought in again. And afterward the people moved from Hazeroth and camped in the wilderness of Paran." NKJV

The man - or in this case - the woman became the mission.

Situations can arise where it is necessary to deal with the person with love but confront the sin in their life that is keeping you and them from God's destinations. It's winning the culture wars and developing a culture of love and honor in the church or ministry that produces long-term success. My prayer for you is that you win the culture war and experience long-term success in your church and ministry.

My eldest son, Justin, who has many years of experience in the marketplace as a businessman, executive pastor and mayor, has some interesting insights concerning culture. He says if we asked any businessperson or organizational leader what the ingredients for a thriving organization are, we would certainly get an array of answers. Some might stay strategy; some will point to the organizational structure, while others would say talent recruitment, overall funding, momentum, staff motivation, marketing plans, etc.

While all of these things are important to a thriving organization, he contends that the key ingredient for a successful organization is a healthy culture. When talking about organizational health and future trajectory, culture trumps all.

This famous quote from legendary business management consultant and writer Peter Drucker—Culture eats strategy for breakfast—sums it up. You can't out strategize a bad organizational culture. To be clear, he didn't mean that strategy was unimportant - rather that a powerful and empowering culture was a surer route to organizational success. In short, successful leaders prioritize and are intentional about the culture (internal and external) of the organization that they lead.

So, who establishes culture? We do. We have to own it. The definition of culture is "the customs, arts, social institutions, and achievements of a particular group or organization." Whether we want to believe it or not, no matter where we are, we step into and out of diverse cultures all day, every day. On any given day, we go from our home culture to our work culture, to the grocery store culture, back to our home and every step in between. All of these places have an established culture. Every group of people, organization, and place you enter has a culture, whether it was intentionally established and recognized or not.

Some cultures are defined unintentionally, and others are more intentional. Have you ever compared the feeling you get when you visit Disney World? How about a typical car dealership? Compare and contrast the Chick-Fil-La experiences to any other fast-food experience. Every home has a different culture. Different households do and say things differently. What we tolerate, what we allow, what we say and how we say it can shape our culture.

The culture that we are in at any given moment often defines what is and what is not acceptable, approved, or appreciated. How you function in that setting, what you say, how you say it, how you react, how you respond, all of it creates our organizational culture. It is like an unspoken rulebook for the space that we are in.

The bottom line is we must define and establish a healthy culture and then commit to operating it. You and your organization are defined by that same culture. Define your culture, because it defines you. The people that visit your home, your business, or your church will consciously or unconsciously, recognize the atmosphere that you have established within your family / team / staff, and in their minds, it will define you.

We will be known by what we say, what we do, how we say it, and how we do it. That goes for how we interact with visitors, members, volunteers, kids, and the community. Most importantly, it shows how we interact with one another.

I ask you to evaluate the culture that you have established, intentionally or not, and prayerfully consider changes that need to be made. Address issues directly and swiftly with your teams and make a commitment to establish a set of cultural commitments for your organization. Document these commitments and keep them in front of your team so that they can seriously consider how they should respond to them to implement a healthy culture into their ministry environment. Below are the cultural commitments that our ministry, staff and volunteers have committed to. Feel free to borrow any or all of these and make them your own.

Put God First

I will put God first in all areas of my life-marriage, family, finances and career.

Make It Better

What am I doing today to improve my church? Can I honestly say I'm doing my best to have excellence in ministry, putting my best foot forward so to speak?

Palms Up

I will own my position's responsibility as long as it's within my care and I will stay mentally ready to release it.

(Sit in a chair with your upward facing palms, resting on your knees to answer hard questions. This act helps you remain calm, honest, and accurate. It is difficult to be angry with anyone while sitting with your palms up.)

Stay Positive

How do I manage the tension triggered by new ideas, innovation and change? Speak blessings, not curses. Say yes as often as possible.

Stay Healthy

How am I taking care of myself spiritually, physically, financially, emotionally, and relationally? How I conduct myself personally in all of these areas affects everyone.

Be Involved

How am I regularly participating in and investing in our mission, ministries and events? Go beyond a job description and know that you are a representative of your church wherever you go.

1+1 >2 (Synergy)

Where am I leveraging talent and skill outside my area of ministry? Do I ask for help from other staff members when needed? Am I willing to receive help when needed?

Give Trust

How much trust do I give to myself and others when I have hesitations? I trust God in you and me. Trust is the firm belief in the reliability, truth, ability, or strength of someone or something.

Love People

How am I overcoming my issues and judgments of others to love people?

Fulfill My Destiny

What am I doing to fulfill God's destiny for my life?

E + R = O: Event + Response = Outcome

My response will determine the outcome.

These are valuable concepts for developing a culture of love and honor in your church and ministry. I encourage you to evaluate, explore, and experiment with them. I think you will be delighted with the results.

My hope for myself and for you is that we will be known for the love and the honor we show people.

SIX

THEY CALL ME THEIR LEADER

NAVIGATING THROUGH THE CHALLENGES OF RAISING UP LEADERS

We only have two choices. We become a one-man show, or we raise up leaders, either we do it all alone or we raise up leaders. Becoming a one-man show is not the best choice. Have you ever seen a one-man band at the state fair or a carnival? You know the guy who is playing the guitar, singing, blowing into a harmonica, beating the drums with his foot, and playing the symbols with his knees all at the same time? He is a one-man band. That guy wears out fast, and it's exhausting watching him do it.

The best decision you will ever make for maximum effectiveness in your ministry is to raise up leaders. Raise them up, train them up, call them out and release them into the work of the ministry. There is however an order to their release and this is the order. We start by challenging them to rise to the occasion, we train them in the principles of leadership, we call them out at the appropriate time and then we release them to come alongside us.

It's true that large churches have the ability to hire people from the outside to serve in staff positions. Those large churches have the resources and a vetting process as well. They usually have a human resources department that can place and remove people, as necessary. Small church pastors usually do not have that option.

Maybe you have a small church or are developing a para-church ministry that barely has enough people to call it a church or ministry. Maybe you are building a church or ministry that is attracting people and it is time for you to raise up leaders due to the ministry needs you have and the growth you are experiencing.

In either scenario, if you are not planning on being a one-man band you need to raise up leaders. Hopefully, this chapter will give you some insights and some proven ways to raise leaders.

There are many good books written on this subject, but what I'll be sharing are some personal insights, as a small church pastor. I will also be sharing some leadership thoughts from my pastor, who has faced this challenge and has been successful at developing and releasing many great leaders of churches and para-church ministries who are impacting the Kingdom all over the world.

I will start by sharing what my pastor of 36 years says on this topic. Pastor Olen Griffing, senior pastor of Shady Grove Church in Grand Prairie, Texas before retirement.

"These are questions I asked myself and things I did in

almost every case. We were small when I started training. I requested and trusted them to train others as we expanded and grew. I desired that each one would have someone they were training to be a leader all the time. I wanted them to know that just because we train someone to be in a staff position, does not mean they are a leader in any situation or calling. I asked myself these questions and expected those I was raising up to do the same.

Personal Discernment

Did they have my heart and were they in agreement with the vision? I'd go out to eat with them or spend time with them to discern their spirit. Did I feel washed out after meeting them? Then something was wrong. I'd inquire about his family's health. If I felt anything negative about these things, I would find a nice way of backing off.

Group relationships reveal areas of need or improvement

Find ways to spend time together, I asked that we all meet at 7am, usually on Tuesday mornings, to play some sport that was team related like volleyball, "slaughter" ball, or softball. Sometimes we have to pitch washers or some other inside game. You can hardly imagine what attitudes will come out while playing competitive sports and games. We would only play an hour so they could get dressed for work. We must build a community spirit among us.

When we were really small, I gathered the five recognized leaders together for a morning meeting in a small room. I said to them, 'We are not growing'. I told them that the average size of an evangelical protestant church in America was 65 people that past year.

There were five of us. If one could get 65 members, then five could cause our church to reach 325 if we give ourselves to prayer, the Word, and worship. I promised them when we begin growing, I would not hog the praise and success but would pass it around. We circled, extending our hands, as we formed a circle of commitment and prayer. From that moment on, we began to reach others.

Just about two years later, we started the first night of teaching First Principles and 400 people began the 42-week course. There were seven weeks on each subject. We had seven lessons, each six weeks long. We required each teacher to have an assistant teacher to train. This is just one example of approved leaders training others.

Each elder would have one or more they were training, according to this pattern. We started with me being the one and only elder. I discipled an elder then both of us discipled another elder. All the while we were meeting and praying. The next thing you know we had twelve elders. They each continued to disciple another elder. They each continued to disciple someone. So, the elders became the base of discipling and training. We allowed some of the ones being trained to bring them to the elders' 7:00 am games.

The elders (with no one else) met weekly to report and plan. An elder was over each department of the church. For example, we had education (teaching), worship, the poor, missions, finances, and evangelism.

We had three elders' retreats annually. Spring was on worship, summer was with our wives, and fall was missions/visions for the next year.

The strength of training leaders was the commitment from each to draw one person alongside. It's hard to explain, but this process produced a voluntary accountability that continued in other leaders as we grew. We started with a small group of leaders training others.

Additionally, once a month we had a "needs night" meeting. This really helped us to develop community among us. I wanted us to be more like a family but with needed organization to meet our growing needs."

-Pastor Olen Griffing

I thought about titling this chapter, "Maximum Effectiveness," because I believe raising up leaders has the power to maximize our effectiveness for the Kingdom.

No doubt some of us may be very gifted at raising up potential leaders in our church or ministry, but some of us may not have a clue as to how to do this. I can relate very well to you and where you are. I had to learn the hard way.

For example, I learned we don't set someone in as an elder just because he is our friend and because he seems spiritually mature and supports us. This kind of decision will cost us our friendship and possibly several members of our church.

I learned some people have an anointing to serve, but not to lead. This decision has the potential for offense and all the hassle that comes with it. I learned the hard way that strong leaders, who attract a following, can pull people away and gather them to him/herself, like King David's son, Absalom.

I have learned so many things the hard way and have suffered many setbacks as a result. But I've also learned that hard lessons are often the best teachers to learn from and hopefully you can learn from someone who learned the hard way, so you don't have to.

I have learned that, as Pastor Olen commented, leadership must have your heart, and some will, while others won't. I have learned that there really are sons and daughters of the house we can raise up for maximum effectiveness. I have also learned we can raise up solid, faithful, trustworthy leaders who have our heart, but it takes time and process to accomplish this.

So, here's my process of raising up leaders for maximum effectiveness in our churches and ministries. My process begins with believing in people. I believe in people. Regardless of their faults, flaws, or maturity level, I believe in people. God has a destination for the men and women He puts on my heart to develop into leaders.

First Samuel speaks about King David's mighty men in this way.

1 Samuel 22:2 "And everyone who was in distress, everyone who was in debt, and everyone who was discontented gathered to him. So, he became captain over them. And there were about four hundred men with him." NKJV

David's mighty men turned out to be amazing and gifted leaders who did incredible exploits. My process begins with believing in those people who God puts on my heart to raise up as leaders. Then I look for faithfulness to God, to the church, and to me as their pastor.

2 Timothy 2:2 "And the things that you have heard from me among many witnesses, commit these to faithful men who will be able to teach others also." NKJV

I'll often give them a ministry opportunity just to see what they will do with it. Faithfulness is only proven when tested, just like submission, or love. These things are only proven when tested.

I look for gifting. Some people have natural giftings for certain areas of ministry. Those gifts may be hidden for some reason but once they are discovered and put to use, they can maximize the effectiveness of the ministry. I have discovered that people find immense joy in serving in areas of ministry where their gifts and talents are being put to use for God's glory.

I've also learned the hard way that when we put people in positions of authority that don't have the gifting, it can cause problems and disappointments. As bad as some people may want to be in a position of leadership when they don't have the gifting, in most cases doesn't work. When they don't have the gifting, the ministry they are leading is often unsuccessful. It's just a matter of time before the man becomes the mission and you have to confront the problem. It's far better to recognize gifting and challenge them to step up than to put them in a position and hope the gifting is there.

So, in my process for raising up leadership, I look for gifting, faithfulness, and submission to authority. As I said earlier, submission is only proven when tested. Are they submitted? We are not looking for "yes" men and women. If our choices are based on agreeable people, we have a flaw in our character and ministry. We are looking for those who will submit to the direction we give them. We're looking for leaders who will trust us, even if they disagree with us, they trust us in spite of what they believe or feel about the decisions we are making on behalf of the ministry. Will they trust us? Will they complete the task we give them wholeheartedly? Sadly, some will, and some will not. Lack of submission is a deal breaker and must be confronted in the hope of winning them, but if not, the mission becomes the man.

I also look for a person who has a servant's heart. My focus is not on their qualifications, their maturity level or even their character flaws. My focus is on do they have a servant's heart? Do they just want to serve? Do they just want to serve the Lord, the church, the ministry and you as their pastor or ministry leader? These people are our greatest asset to maximizing our effectiveness. Maturity can come through education, character flaws can be addressed and repented of, and qualifications can be developed, but becoming a servant is an issue of the heart and Jesus makes that very clear in the New Testament.

Mark 9:35 "And He sat down, called the twelve, and

said to them, 'If anyone desires to be first, he shall be last of all and servant of all'." NKJV

All the things I have mentioned require a relationship to be developed between us and our potential leaders. As Pastor Olen spoke about earlier, raising up leaders must be relational. First and foremost, believe in the people God put on your heart as potential leaders and begin to build relationships with those people. Spend time with them, pray with them, and hang out with them. Speak life into them and challenge them. Begin to call them out and upward. Help them see what God sees in them. Help them to believe in themselves, regardless of their past or current situations. Help them to recognize their gifting and give them ministry opportunities that will stretch and challenge them.

It's through spending time with these potential leaders that we can recognize pride issues, submission issues, or faith issues. Spending time with them will give us an opportunity to speak into their lives so that transformation can take place. Whether they understand it or not, their hope as future leaders is you. So go after what God is after in their lives. Do it lovingly, with grace and mercy, but go after it. Their success is dependent on them giving God what He is after in their lives, whether that is sin, pride or faith issues. Giving God what He is after is the key to their success in life and ministry.

If we can't speak into their lives and bring adjustments where needed, we are wasting our time and theirs. Call out what God has revealed to you, for their sake, and for both of your maximum effectiveness.

Lastly, in my process of raising up potential leaders, I like to challenge them with a question. The answer to this one question tells me so much of what I need to know about them and their potential as future leaders. I ask them if they could do anything for God, and they were not limited by time, education, or finances, what would it be?

I ask the question, if they could do anything they wanted to do in the church, in the marketplace, mission field or wherever for the Lord, whether it be evangelism, discipleship, marketplace ministry, children's ministry, youth ministry, mission work, leadership, preaching, teaching, singing, playing an instrument on the worship team, if they could do anything they wanted to do for the Lord, what would it be?

When they answer, I tell them their answer is their *spiritual passion* and their spiritual passion did not come from the devil, or even their own imagination. That spiritual passion comes from the Lord, and it has everything to do with their calling and giftings, and God's vision for their life. Helping them discover their spiritual passion and helping them accomplish it maximizes our effectiveness and theirs.

To finish this chapter, let's address friendships. Though they call us their leader, they may not call us their friend and we have to be okay with that. Not every leader we raise up will see us as a close friend, nor will we consider them our close friend. However, a great need in our life as a pastor or a ministry leader is to have a friend who is as close as a brother. Every pastor and leader needs a friend but sadly, according to the statistics, most don't have any. And for this reason, many leave the ministry.

Now let me define what a friend is, based upon what I believe every pastor needs.

A friend is:

1.Someone who has your back right or wrong. They stick with us through thick and thin, the good, the bad, and the ugly of ministry.

2.A truth speaker who, in love, tells us when we are wrong. They will say things that we may not want to hear, but we need to hear.

3.A loyal person when no one else is and loyalty is only proven when tested.

4.Someone who will support us when no one else does. This includes moral support, prayer support, and financial support.

5.Someone we can just be our self around. You can just be you without having to wear our ministry hat or act like a spiritual leader who has it all together.

6.Someone who loves us past our character flaws and personal struggles. Usually, it's a good friend that knows our greatest weakness.

7.A person who replenishes us and does not drain us. We should always have people in our lives that replenish us mentally, emotionally, and spiritually. Every pastor needs a friend who has these qualities.

In addition, every pastor needs someone who will

challenge them to come up higher in their relationship with God and His calling upon their life. This can be a friend, a spiritual mother or father, even spiritual brothers and sisters. Ministry leadership can be lonely. Having a friend can be the difference between success and failure in both our life and ministry. My hope and prayer for you is that if they call you their leader, they also call you their friend.

SEVEN
THEY CALL ME A FIREMAN
NAVIGATING THROUGH THE CHALLENGES OF CONFLICT

I contemplated titling this chapter, "The Art of Putting out Fires."

Be aware that anytime we have people involved in serving our church or ministry, there will be opportunities for offense.

Matthew 18:7 "Woe to the world because of offenses! For offenses must come, but woe to that man by whom the offense comes!" NKJV

Romans 16:17 "Now I urge you, brethren, note those who cause divisions and offenses, contrary to the doctrine which you learned, and avoid them." NKJV

Offenses can be the result of sin issues, personality differences, character flaws and differences of opinion. The real problem is the unwillingness of people to love each other past those offenses. As pastors and leaders, we wear the hat of the fireman. We find ourselves having to put out fires and deal with people who have an offense against someone in our church or ministry.

There are many good books on this subject, and perhaps you've already learned a lot from the fires you've already had to extinguish. The truth is that offenses must be dealt with, because a fire only smolders if not completely put out. People often hold onto an offense for years, sometimes even taking it to their grave. They either keep it to themselves letting the fire smolder, or ignite others through their criticism, causing them to take on the offense. Offenses must be dealt with.

For those of you like me, who hate confrontation; ask yourself if you value the health and success of your ministry more than you hate confrontation. If the answer is yes, settle it, because as a leader, you have to protect your ministry from division and strife, which is a demonic strategy from the pits of hell to destroy your ministry.

Most offenses can be resolved just by getting the two parties together and communicating as Christians. Often, one person doesn't even know they did anything to offend the other. It is good to give opportunity for the offended person to voice their concern and hear the other person.

Matthew 18:15 -17 "Moreover if your brother sins against you, go and tell him about his fault between you and him alone. If he hears you, you have gained your brother. But if he will not hear, take with you one or two more, that by the mouth of two or three witnesses every word may be established. And if he refuses to hear them, tell it to the church. But if he refuses even to hear the

church, let him be to you like a heathen and a tax collector."
NKJV

Scripturally there is a three-step process for offense. The
first step requires those who are offended to go to the
person that offended them. The second step is to bring
someone with us if we are unsuccessful in resolving the
issue. The third step is to take the situation before the
church.

A pastor friend of mine recently pointed out to me that
too often we skip step one and go right to step two or three.
People who get offended at someone often feel the need to
take a witness with them to confront someone or spread the
news around the church.

As a fireman, I have found that often step one resolves
the conflict and brings healing to the relationship. The
challenge is holding the offended person accountable and to
take step one first. As spiritual leaders, we need to ensure
they approach the person they are offended by to try to
resolve the conflict with that person alone.

I tell my staff and ministry leaders that if they are
offended by something someone has said or done, they
should first seek to resolve it with the Lord. If that doesn't
clear the offense, they need to address it directly with the
person involved. If that doesn't clear it, I encourage them to
continue to follow the scriptural path in Matthew 18. I have
found this approach to be very successful, and it has
become a core part of the culture within our leadership
team and church.

There are offenses that burn so deeply they require a lot

more work to extinguish. As a fireman, I have three objectives in mind to extinguish these deep smoldering offenses.

My first objective is to get all the cards on the table, so nothing is left smoldering. What happened? What was said? What was done? What should have been done? What should have been said? It's only when the two parties fully understand each other's perspective that we move forward. If this doesn't happen, the fire still smolders and will reignite at the littlest spark.

James 5:16 "Confess your trespasses to one another, and pray for one another, that you may be healed. The effective, fervent prayer of a righteous man avails much." NKJV

Getting all the cards on the table exposes the offending flames for both parties to see.

My second objective is to help each party recognize what they may not see. I try my best to help them understand the other's perspective. I want them to understand why they were hurt and why they feel the way they feel. Understanding can be like water on the flame. Understanding brings clarity, allowing us to see beyond the smoke of a burning offense. I like to let people talk about their offense, not vent, but talk about how they feel. I have discovered this will often lead to repentance, forgiveness, and restoration. Restoration is your ultimate goal, but some fires burn so hot they have to be extinguished through forgiveness. Forgiveness must take place before restoration can be obtained.

My third objective is to bring revelation about scriptural

forgiveness. This is where the two parties forgive each other, and the flames go out. I use the term scriptural forgiveness for a reason. Scriptural forgiveness is the kind of forgiveness Jesus gives us, but so often we do not give to each other. Too often our forgiveness is like the world's forgiveness, or it's a forgiveness based upon our own definition that is not scriptural.

In some cases, offended people can harden their hearts and refuse to forgive. The wound can be so deep they just can't see themselves ever forgiving the person who hurt them. One of the greatest challenges we face as pastors and leaders is convincing people to forgive scripturally. My process for doing this involves helping them see how unforgiveness and forgiveness can impact their lives.

First, I show them how forgiveness empowers them to stand confident before God.

Matthew 6:9-15 "In this manner, therefore, pray: Our Father in heaven, Hallowed be Your name. Your kingdom comes. Your will be done on earth as it is in heaven. Give us this day our daily bread. And forgive us our debts, as we forgive our debtors. And do not lead us into temptation but deliver us from the evil one. For Yours is the kingdom and the power and the glory forever. Amen. For if you forgive men their trespasses, your heavenly Father will also forgive you. But if you do not forgive men their trespasses, neither will your father forgive your trespasses." NKJV

In this passage trespasses are also translated as a fault, offense, or sin. This passage also tells us that unforgiveness can affect our eternal future. So, the question arises, what happens to us when we are standing before God at the judgment seat of Christ, and we have been harboring unforgiveness toward someone? We have not forgiven someone who trespassed against us or sinned against us. What happens to us when we are standing before God, knowing we refused to forgive, and the Father says because you refuse to forgive them, I refuse to forgive you? What happens to us if our sins are not forgiven? What happens next? I don't want to find out, do you?

In my mind, what some person did to me is not worth finding out! What some church member did to me is not worth finding out. What my father or mother did or didn't do for me is not worth finding out. Whatever some relative, boss, coworker, friend or pastor who did something that hurt me, it's just not worth it to me to find out. I'm not saying it can rob us of our salvation. I'm saying that I'm not willing to find out how it affects my eternal future. How about you?

I want to stand confident before the Lord at the judgment seat of Christ. I want to hear Him say, "Well done, good and faithful servant. Enter into the joy of the Lord," not, "What were you thinking?"

Forgiveness empowers us to stand confidently before the Lord. I believe that unforgiveness is the greatest sin in the church today. It's not gossip, backbiting, judging each other, or even people causing division and strife. The greatest sin and most destructive sin in the church today, is unforgiveness.

The Lord did not say if we gossip our sins will not be

forgiven. He did not say if we judge someone our sins will not be forgiven. Nor did He say if we cause division and strife, our sins will not be forgiven. He said if we don't forgive others their sins against us, our sins will not be forgiven. Therefore, unforgiveness is the most destructive sin in the church. The reason is that people justify it.

I have had many conversations with people harboring unforgiveness, saying, "Well, Pastor, this is what so and so did or said to me. Pastor, they're my brother, or my sister, and I'm supposed to love them in the Lord but I'm not about to forgive them for what they did or said to me."

They believe their unforgiveness is justified. Maybe some business deal went south, or someone said something ugly to them, or they were in a relationship that broke up, or someone else was picked for the church play over them or said or did something they disagree with. In their mind, their unforgiveness is justified and suddenly a root of bitterness springs up.

Hebrews 12:14-15 "Pursue peace with all people, and holiness, without which no one will see the Lord: Looking carefully, lest anyone fall short of the grace of God; lest any root of bitterness springing up cause trouble, and by this many become defiled; a root of bitterness begins with unforgiveness and ends with defilement of many people." NKJV

The Greek word "defiled" means "to dye with another color, to stain, to defile, pollute, contaminate." Unforgiveness is like putting a drop of food coloring in a glass of clear water. It's now polluted, stained, and contaminated. It's transformed from something created to be pure into something polluted or defiled.

Verse 14 says, without which no one will see the Lord. As a fireman, I like to ask people who are unwilling to forgive, this question, "Do you want to one day see the Lord?" I tell them that I know when I go to heaven; I want to be able to see the Lord. I don't want to miss an opportunity to see the Lord Jesus in the beauty realms of heaven. When I ask them that question, they always answer "yes."

1 John 4:20 "If someone says, 'I love God,' and hates his brother, he is a liar; for he who does not love his brother whom he has seen, how can he love God whom he has not seen?" NKJV

I ask people the question, "Do you love God?" Do you ever say to someone, "I just love the Lord!" I ask them, "Do you hate anyone? Because if you say you love the Lord, but you are harboring hate in your heart toward someone, the word of God calls you a liar, and there is a desperate need for forgiveness toward those people you hate."

Ephesians 4:30 -32 "And do not grieve the Holy Spirit of God, by whom you were sealed for the day of redemption. Let all bitterness, wrath, anger, clamor, and evil speaking be put away from you, with all malice. And be kind to one another, tenderhearted, forgiving one another, even as God in Christ forgave you." NKJV

If you need a reason to forgive, here it is. Christ forgave you. According to scripture, "to forgive," means to be gracious, to be kind, to pardon, to restore. So unforgiveness would be to refuse to pardon, refuse to be kind, refuse to be gracious and refuse to restore. There are a lot of things that can produce a root of bitterness, such as abandonment, rejection, infidelity, disloyalty, molestation and abuse. Any type of violation that devastates you mentally, physically, or emotionally can produce a root of bitterness.

Forgiveness is the ax we use to chop that root. Forgiveness is all about letting go of the past so we can have an abundant life in the future. We can't drive our car forward looking in the rearview mirror. We have to look out the windshield to see the Lord's vision for our future.

I say to people, "I don't know if you are harboring unforgiveness towards anyone, but the Holy Spirit does. Maybe He's whispering in your ear the name of a person you need to forgive. Have you forgiven them? Is there hate in your heart toward them? Are you defiled by your unforgiveness? It's time to let go. It's time to set them free so you can be free." Forgiveness is a big deal to God. Let's read this passage again.

Matthew 6:15 "But if you do not forgive men their trespasses, neither will your Father forgive your trespasses." NKJV

The Lord did not say that about murder. He did not say that about adultery. He did not say that about divorce, stealing, lust, or anger. The Lord did not say if we commit adultery, if we kill someone, lust after someone, or steal something, our sins are not forgiven. He did not say this about any other sin, except unforgiveness. Forgiveness empowers us to stand confidently before the Lord. I tell people forgiveness is a powerful tool for creating success in their life. Forgiveness gives us the power to see mountains removed.

Forgiveness is like one of those huge earth moving bulldozers, so powerful they can literally move mountains. That's how powerful forgiveness is. It moves mountains from our path. They are the mountains that keep us from success. They are the mountains standing in our way of the Lord's blessing.

Mark 11:22 -24 "So Jesus answered and said to them, 'Have faith in God. For assuredly, I say to you, whoever says to this mountain, be removed and be cast into the sea, and does not doubt in his heart, but believes that those things he says will be done, he will have whatever he says. Therefore, I say to you, whatever things you ask when you pray, believe that you receive them, and you will have them'." NKJV

Jesus is saying to have faith to speak to the mountains. God is a mountain moving God. We see throughout scripture where He parts the Red Sea, slays Goliath, heals the sick, raises the dead and calms the storm. Our God is a mountain moving God. Releasing our faith removes the mountains that are holding us back from success.

But look what the Lord says in the very next verse.

Mark 11:25-26 "And whenever you stand praying, if you have anything against anyone, forgive him, that your Father in heaven may also forgive you your trespasses. But if you do not forgive, neither will your Father in heaven forgive your trespasses." NKJV

If you have anything against anyone, forgive. Unforgiveness hinders our prayers. Unforgiveness keeps our mountains from being removed and this could be why the mountains in our life don't seem to be going anywhere.

I like to ask people, "How long have you been standing in faith, speaking to those mountains, proclaiming God's power in your situation? Has the mountain moved? Has the giant fallen? Has the storm calmed?"

Forgiveness gives us the power to see mountains removed. It cranks up that mountain moving bulldozer. So, when I am forced to be a fireman, I tell people forgiveness is a powerful tool in creating success in their life and forgiveness is a powerful weapon against the onslaught of the demonic forces.

Ephesians 6:12 "For we do not wrestle against flesh and blood, but against principalities, against powers, against the rulers of the darkness of this age, against spiritual hosts of wickedness in the heavenly places." NKJV

There is a war raging and we're in a fight, whether we realize it or not. There is a demonic realm out there, strategizing and scheming to rob us of our faith, our physical, emotional, and mental health, and overall well-being. He is an enemy who is set on the destruction of our marriage, family, finances, and ministry. Without question, he is after every area of our life.

Don't think for a minute that we're not in a fight for the well-being of our soul and the abundant life Jesus came to give us. The question is, "Does the enemy have an open door into our life, and if so, how do we shut it? Do you remember the story of the man who owned a debt he could not pay in Matthew, Chapter 18? It was equivalent to millions of dollars, and he was brought before the master, begging for forgiveness.

The Lord forgave him that huge debt and set him free. The story was an analogy of the Lord forgiving our debt and setting us free. Remember what that man did? He went out and found someone who owed him a relatively small debt and he refused to forgive that debt and had him thrown in prison.

Matthew 18:21-35 "Then Peter came to Him and said, 'Lord, how often shall my brother sin against me, and I forgive him? Up to seven times?' Jesus said to him, 'I do not say to you, up to seven times, but up to seventy times seven. Therefore, the kingdom of heaven is like a certain king who wanted to settle accounts with his servants. And when he had begun to settle accounts, one was brought to him who owed him ten thousand talents. But as he was not able to pay, his master commanded that he be sold, with his wife and children and all that he had, and that payment be made. The servant therefore fell down before him, saying, 'Master, have patience with me, and I will pay you all.' Then the master of that servant was moved with compassion, released him, and forgave him the debt. But that servant went out and found one of his fellow servants who owed him a hundred denarii; and he laid hands on him and took him by the throat, saying, 'Pay me what you owe!' So, his fellow servant fell down at his feet and begged him, saying, 'Have patience with me, and I will pay you all.' And he would not, but went and threw him into prison till he should pay the debt. So, when his fellow servants saw what had been done, they were very grieved and came and told their master all that had been done. Then his master, after he had called him, said to him, 'You wicked servant! I forgave you all that debt because you begged me. Should you not also have had compassion on your fellow servant, just as I had pity on you?' And his master was angry and delivered him to the torturers until he should pay all that was due to him. So, my heavenly Father also will do to you if each of you, from his heart, does not forgive his brother his trespasses'." NKJV

The context of the story is forgiveness. Peter asked how often must one forgive. The Lord is speaking to His disciples about forgiveness, about this huge debt that was pardoned and what happens when we refuse to forgive others.

Matthew 18:34 "And his master was angry and delivered him to the torturers until he should pay all that was due to him." NKJV

Your translation may use the word *tormentor*. According to some theologians, the word tormentors probably means, *keepers of the prisons*. Torments were inflicted on criminals, not on debtors. They were inflicted by stretching the limbs, or pinching the flesh, or putting out the eyes, or taking off the skin while alive, etc. It is not probable that anything of this kind is intended, but only that the servant was punished by imprisonment until the debt should be paid.

Now, let me ask you something. Who is the tormentor?

Who is the tormentor of our soul? Who is the one who oppresses us, brings depression into our life, and robs us of joy, peace and faith? It's Satan and the demonic realm. Unforgiveness gives Satan an open door to torment us. He has legal grounds, and the Lord gives him the authority to do it.

Matthew 18:35 "So my heavenly Father also will do to you if each of you, from his heart, does not forgive his brother his trespasses." NKJV

Unforgiveness is a heart issue, and it is in the heart where forgiveness must take place. I know of people who are tormented night and day because of unforgiveness. When they see the person that hurt them or hear their name, something comes all over them such as anger and frustration. They go to bed thinking about that person and what they did to them. They wake up thinking about what that person did to them. They are tormented. Satan has them in prison. Bound up, pinching their flesh, poking them in the eye. The Lord gives him the authority to do it.

God loves us enough to allow the devil to torment us until we come to that place where we choose to forgive from our heart. We have to understand that forgiveness is for us so we can be whole, healthy, and free, no longer tormented, defiled and unable to experience the abundant life Jesus came to give us. Forgiveness is for us so we can see our mountains removed and experience the success that God intends for our life. It is so we can stand confidently before the Lord in our eternal future. As firemen we must show people how to forgive someone scripturally in order to put out the flames once and for all.

Ephesians 4:30 -32 "And do not grieve the Holy Spirit of God, by whom you were sealed for the day of redemption. Let all bitterness, wrath, anger, clamor, and evil speaking be put away from you, with all malice. And be kind to one another, tenderhearted, forgiving one another, even as God in Christ forgave you. Instead, be kind to each other, tenderhearted, forgiving one another, just as God through Christ has forgiven you." NLT

The Greek words for *just as* means *even as, in proportion as, in the degree that*. Our conclusion is this. We forgive others like God forgives us. We know this is true because that word "forgive" in Matthew 14-15, is the same word, which means to send away, to bid going away or to let go, give a debt, or forgive. When our sins are forgiven the Lord says, "See ya." He lets it go. He doesn't say, "See you later." We tend to hang on instead of letting go. Instead of saying, "See ya," we say, "See you later."

Scriptural forgiveness is forgiving others the same way God forgives us.

What does that look like? What does forgiving the same way God forgives us look like in our lives? Scriptural forgiveness requires five actions.

Actions produce results. The results we are looking for is the abundant life in Christ, the blessed life, the fullness of life. We seek to stand confidently before God, witnessing mountains being removed that block our success as we achieve victory over the demonic forces that torment us due to unforgiveness. Scriptural forgiveness requires five actions.

1. Scriptural forgiveness requires death.

To forgive someone scripturally, we must die. Jesus died so we can be forgiven. The death we suffer is the death of our own flesh. It's death to self. It is dying to our hurt feelings or our anger issues or maybe our woundedness. It's dying to everything in us that wants to rise up, attack, or get revenge. It is dying to everything in us that wants to hurt those who hurt us, abuse those who abuse us, either physically or verbally. To forgive scripturally, we must die to our flesh. Let it be crucified. It's the cross. We bear the burden of the crucified life we live. Jesus said, "Pick up your cross and follow Me."

Galatians 2:20 "I have been crucified with Christ. It is no longer I who live, but Christ who lives in me. And the life I now live in the flesh I live by faith in the Son of God who loved me and gave himself for me." NLT

We say, "I forgive them," but I'm still mad at them. I'm still angry at them. I want to see them suffer like I suffered. As a matter of fact, I hope they die. All the flesh in us rises up and God sees it. Sound familiar? Aren't you glad Jesus didn't say, "I forgive you but I'm not willing to die for you. I forgive you but I'm still mad at you, I'm still angry at you, I want you to suffer like I suffered because of your sin." Aren't you glad Jesus didn't say I forgive you but I'm not willing to be crucified for you? Where would we be had Jesus not been willing to die for us?

As firemen we must ask people if they are willing to die

to their flesh so they can be recognized by God as someone who truly forgives others, just as He has forgiven them. We have to ask are they willing to die to the flesh so they can experience the abundant life in Christ. To forgive as Jesus forgives, I must die as He died. Scriptural forgiveness requires death.

2. Scriptural forgiveness chooses to forget.

Psalm103:12 "He has removed our sins as far from us as the east is from the west." NLT

Hebrews 8:12 "for I will be merciful to their unrighteousness, and their sins and their lawless deeds I will remember no more." NKJV

Scriptural forgiveness chooses to remember no more. This doesn't mean the Lord can't remember, He just chooses not to. The Lord chooses to remember His grace, His mercy, and His forgiveness.

We tend to say that I forgive them, but I'm never going to forget what they did. Sound familiar? Aren't you glad Jesus didn't say I forgive you but I'm never going to forget what you did? Can you see Jesus up in heaven, dwelling on it, tormented by it? It's weighing on Him, oppressing Him. He's depressed by it. He even has bad dreams over it. No, absolutely not.

Pastors and ministry leaders, we must help people understand that forgiveness is a choice. We choose to remember no more. We choose to forget about it when it comes to mind. It's not that we don't remember. It's just that it's healed, and no longer affects us. It has no power over us. It doesn't hurt anymore because we chose to forgive. We can choose to dwell on what they did, or we can choose to dwell on the forgiveness God has shown us.

The devil can't play with a healed memory. The tormentors can't torment a healed memory. This is why allowing the Holy Spirit to heal our memories is so important. If our memories are not healed, it's an open door for depression. To forgive as Jesus forgave, I must choose to forget. Scriptural forgiveness chooses to forget.

3. Scriptural forgiveness requires no punishment.

We say I forgive them, but I can't wait for God to get them. I forgive them but I can't wait for God to punish them for what they did to me. We say, "Punish them, Lord. Look what they're doing to me. Go get them, God. Bring down fire and brimstone!"

Aren't you glad the Lord didn't say that He forgave you but He can't wait for the Father to get you? It's interesting to me that King David cried to God to punish his enemies, and he was not allowed to build the temple, the place of God's manifest presence because he was a man of war and shed so much blood.

1 Chronicles 28:3 "But God said to me, 'You shall not build a house for My name, because you have been a man of war and have shed blood'." NLT

I've always wondered how often people miss entering into the presence of the Lord because of unforgiveness and a heart that desires punishment for others. God poured out His entire wrath on Jesus. Aren't you glad?

Job said in Job 31:30: "No, I have never sinned by cursing anyone or by asking for revenge." NLT

Job saw asking for revenge as a sin. On the other hand, we have a tendency to hope something bad happens to them. We have a tendency to curse them with our words. We may hope for the worst for them, though we may not say it.

"We know we have forgiven someone when we're driving down the road and we see that person pulled over by the highway patrol, getting a ticket, and you don't laugh!"*

To forgive as Jesus forgave, I must not require punishment. Scriptural forgiveness requires no punishment.

4. Scriptural forgiveness seeks restoration.

The fourth action we take in walking in scriptural forgiveness is seeking restoration. Our challenge is to help people who are harboring unforgiveness understand this truth.

Christians will say I forgive them but never want to have anything to do with them. I forgive them, but I don't ever want to see them again. I don't want to talk to them. I don't want them calling me up. I don't want to hear from them. I don't even want to think about them.

Aren't you glad Jesus didn't say, "I forgive you, but I don't ever want to have anything to do with you?" I forgive you but I don't ever want to see you. I don't want to hear from you. I don't want to talk to you. I don't want you calling me up or having anything else to do with you. I don't even want to think about you."

---

* The *Chronicles of Leroy*

Scriptural forgiveness seeks restoration just as the Lord did for us.

The Lord seeks our restoration. When we sin, the Lord seeks to restore our relationship with Him. Ever since the fall of man, the Lord has sought after restoration. Therefore, He sent His only begotten Son so that we might be restored.

Our action is to forgive as God forgave us. The Lord seeks restoration, but He does not force it. Some people in your life will not let restoration take place. They are just too hurt and too bitter. They don't want restoration. Just like a lot of people reject Jesus. They don't want restoration. Our responsibility is to do our part, to open ourselves up to restoration because we have been forgiven.

This takes wisdom because some people may not be healthy for us to be around them even though we have forgiven them. This could be due to their unrepentant sin or bitterness. This could cause destruction in our life.

Years ago, we had a family attending our church that I counseled. The lady told me she had been molested by her father. He never repented to her or asked forgiveness. She thought it was not wise to let her two young girls be around that grandfather. She had forgiven him and sought restoration but used wisdom.

Scriptural forgiveness seeks restoration, but it is contingent upon how destructive that restoration is or can be, not because of us, but because of how broken, sinful and destructive they are. To forgive as Jesus forgave, we must seek restoration. Scriptural forgiveness seeks restoration.

5. Scriptural forgiveness speaks forth blessing.

Aren't you glad Jesus didn't say, "I forgive you but I'm never going to bless you?" Too often we can find ourselves forgiving someone but there is no desire in our hearts to see them blessed in any way by the Lord. However, with the Lord's forgiveness comes His blessing upon our lives. His word speaks forth blessing over us, making our forgiveness complete.

Forgiveness is complete when we are able from our heart to speak forth blessing over people who have hurt or wounded us. Years ago, I was at a prayer meeting with some other ministers from our community, one of which was an old friend, who had caused much harm in my life by what he said and did. As well, I had caused him much harm in his life. Even though we had both forgiven each other for the harm we had caused in each other's lives, it was when I began to bless him that something started to break in our hearts. He just began to weep, and I continued to bless him and his ministry. And he began to bless me as well and from that point on, our relationship was restored. It was a powerful moment in both of our lives, and it released success for both of our churches. To forgive as Jesus forgave, I must bless as He blesses. Scriptural forgiveness speaks forth blessing.

What do you want people to call you? My hope is they call me a minister who forgives scripturally, a lover of God and people, and the fireman when necessary.

EIGHT

THEY CALL ME A BRONC RIDER

NAVIGATING THROUGH THE CHALLENGES OF PASTORING HIGHLY MOTIVATED SUCCESSFUL PEOPLE

Having been around horses most of my life, as well as riding bucking horses in rodeos when I was young, I know that different breeds of horses have unique capabilities according to their breed. For example, draft horses are bred for strength, giving them the ability to work and pull heavy loads. Quarter horses are often bred for working with cattle and other livestock because of their speed and agility. Certain other breeds, such as Arabian horses, are known for their stamina. Even the American Mustang has unique capabilities common to the breed, but can be wild, stubborn, and difficult to break.

This brings us to the thoroughbreds. This breed is known for their high energy and speed. These are the horses that are trained to run in the Kentucky Derby and other famous races around the United States and the world.

These horses are bred to excel in racing, demonstrating unmatched speed and endurance.

I have discovered in my years of ministry that there are times and seasons that the Lord brings thoroughbreds into our church and ministry. Like in our thoroughbred analogy, these are very capable people who run to win. They are highly motivated and successful people with unique capabilities that need to be pastored. These people are motivated by success, whether in the business world or in their work unto the Lord and they are seldom content just being a member or even serving on a team. They are often visionaries themselves and find great purpose and a sense of achievement in creating and accomplishing remarkable things for the Kingdom. These thoroughbreds are often great financial supporters of our churches and they are willing to get behind the vision both in leadership and financial support. Sounds like good news, right? I'll take a stable full of thoroughbreds.

It is good news when the Lord sends us gifted and accomplished people to help us with the work God has called us to do. However, if you have ever been around horses, you know they require a great deal of care and training. Stalls have to be cleaned, the horses have to be fed, watered, groomed, and exercised, as well as trained. The same is true for the thoroughbreds in your ministry. They need both special care and training to win their race. What we're feeding the sheep is not necessarily the right feed for these thoroughbreds. They need a higher-level feed, in addition to care and training. We must understand that God is training them for something unique. God made them highly motivated and successful and along with that comes a unique set of challenges for us as their pastor. It is wise to consider them in this light, just as we regard the people differently who are the workhorses of our congregation and those who are like the Mustang who are wild, stubborn and need to be tamed by the Holy Spirit so they can accomplish mighty things for the Kingdom.

Each people group comes with a unique set of challenges to prepare them for God's calling in their lives, service in the church and ministry in the marketplace. It's interesting to me how many scriptures reference horses, mules, sheep, goats, and other livestock in relation to people.

Psalms 32:9 "Do not be like a senseless horse or mule that needs a bit and bridle to keep it under control." NLT

Matthew 25:32 "All the nations will be gathered before Him, and He will separate them one from another, as a shepherd divides his sheep from the goats." NKJV

Next, we have the challenge of training thoroughbreds. Training involves pouring into them the things that God wants them to hear that will help them to win their race. Spending time with them is extremely important and I encourage that we take and make the time because the race is won at the finish line. We need to train these thoroughbreds in their leadership skills. This can be done through various training methods such as attending conferences, suggesting books, listening to podcasts and to well-known teachers on the subject of leadership. The time we spend with any of these training methods will help us and our thoroughbred to win the race.

In my experience the special feed needed to nourish them frequently relates more to loving their spouse and sacrificing for their family more than any other factor. Their training is often more practical in nature rather than spiritual. Helping them to understand that the two are connected is extremely important.

For example, one of the thoroughbreds the Lord sent to our church became a good friend of mine and served our church for many years. He was ambitious and successful in business and the ministries he was involved in at the church. He was a visionary for the calling of God upon his life and for our church. He was also adept and passionate for the Kingdom. He had accomplished remarkable things in his life and his career. God's call to ministry was a driving force in his life and still is to this day. However, he was missing a vital part of his life that was to value and honor his wife. The greatest need he had was to see her as the helpmate God intended her to be for the deficits in his life. This was a struggle for him and hindered him in many ways, most that he couldn't see.

The good news is, over time, he began to see her in a different light, and he received her as the helpmeet that God intended, making him far more successful in his life and ministry. I believe he will finish well this race we call Christianity.

When training thoroughbreds to win the race, it's often the basic spiritual principles that they need the most. Its things like loving their wives as Christ loved the church, honoring them, and seeing them as treasures from God. Sometimes it's humility, integrity or learning how to show love and gentleness toward people. With others it could be things like caring more for others than we do for ourselves. A common blind spot is not valuing other people's opinion when it differs from our own. Basic practical and spiritual principles are often the greatest need in the life of a thoroughbred.

Ephesians 5:25 "Husbands, love your wives, just as Christ also loved the church and gave Himself for her." NKJV

1 Peter 3:7 "Husbands, likewise, dwell with them with understanding, giving honor to the wife, as to the weaker vessel, and as being heirs together of the grace of life, that your prayers may not be hindered." NKJV

Proverbs 18:22 "The man who finds a wife finds a treasure, and he receives favor from the Lord." NLT

Another important area thoroughbreds need training in is the Lord's timing and process. They often lack patience in waiting upon the Lord and allowing God's timing and process to take place so that they can win. Thoroughbreds are known to get anxious in the gate before the race begins. They are anxious to run out in front ahead of everyone else.

In western vernacular, it's called champing at the bit. They are raring to go. They are eager to get out of the gate and run full speed ahead, but races are won by the jockey controlling the horse's strength and stamina, and setting a pace to win the race. The Lord has both timing and a process that they must understand as He prepares them to win their races.

God has both timing and a process that enables us to accomplish the remarkable things he has called us to do. The same is true for those highly motivated and successful people. The timing relates to God's timetable for what He wants to accomplish through us and the process relates to what God is doing in us. Both are necessary to win the race. It is when we get ahead of God or lag behind, that we find ourselves discouraged. It is when we allow God to do the work in us that He desires to do so that our race is not run in vain. When we fail to let God have what He is after in our lives, the goals and dreams He has given us remain just out of reach and out of the winner's circle.

The Lord's timing and process must be understood to win the race. As pastors and trainers, we must communicate this to our thoroughbreds. When we recognize this process taking place in their lives as thoroughbred trainers, we must speak into that. We must address what we believe God is after in their lives so that they can win their race. When we fail to address the issues that we know the Holy Spirit is after; we do our thoroughbreds a great disservice and hinder them from winning their race. We are not the jockey on the back of the thoroughbreds. That role is for the Holy Spirit. We are simply those training the thoroughbreds to win their race.

It is important for leaders to challenge thoroughbreds to set spiritual goals for their lives, such as developing the ability to hear and discern the voice of the Holy Spirit, become spiritually mature and discover their spiritual passion. Those three goals will impact their lives for success in God's eye and will also ensure success in their marriage and family. If they will be as motivated for personal growth and learning to hear God's voice and discovering their spiritual passion as they are in pursuing success in the marketplace, they will accomplish so much more in life.

There is much to be said on developing spiritual maturity and the ability to discern the voice of the Holy Spirit. There are many good books on these topics. My suggestion would be to read these books with them for input and encouragement.

Discovering their spiritual passion can set them on a course for God's calling in their life and the very purpose for which He created and gifted them. The way I help them discover their spiritual passion is by asking the question I spoke about in an earlier chapter of this book. The question is, "What would you do, if you could do anything for God and you are not limited by time, education, or finances? You could do any type of ministry or service to God that you want, and you were in no way limited by anything, what would you do for God?"

They will often answer that question by saying they would be involved in some type of mission work, marketplace ministry or perhaps teaching or leading a small group. Some answer by saying they would be involved in some type of ministry to the poor or youth, or maybe children. The answer can vary in so many ways. Once they answer that question, I would identify that as their spiritual passion.

The second question I would ask them is, "Where do you think your spiritual passion came from?" It was not something they just thought up because it was the passion of their heart. It certainly was not something that came from the demonic realm. So where did that spiritual passion come from? Obviously, it came from the Lord.

I like to help thoroughbreds discover their spiritual passion and then do everything I can to set them on a course of pursuing it; even if it's in small steps and measures, allowing God's timing and process to take place. I challenge these highly motivated and successful people to reach these three spiritual goals, maturity in Christ, discerning the voice of the Lord and discovering their spiritual passion. As they do this, I believe they will stand in the Winner's Circle at the end of their race. So will you as a Bronc Rider.

Before we move on, I want to acknowledge that we can feel somewhat intimidated by these passionate and accomplished people in our church or ministry. Their success, giftings and even their vision may surpass ours. It is during these times that we must recognize the Lord's purpose in placing them under our leadership. His purpose may be beyond our understanding at the moment, but there is a reason why we have them in our ministry. We are the

Lord's instrument to speak into their lives. Thoroughbreds need pastors as much as anyone else, so as we recognize that it is wise to take our eyes off of ourselves and place them on the Lord and what He wants to do in their lives. Remember when it comes to training those thoroughbreds it's not about us it's about them.

NINE

THEY CALL ME A SHEPHERD

NAVIGATING THROUGH THE LOSS OF YOUR INVESTMENT

One of the most difficult things we go through as pastors is when people leave the church. The people we love and care for. These are people we invest our time, energy and resources in. People we invest countless hours encouraging them and walking with them through the difficulties in their personal lives, marriage and finances. Spending hour after hour, from personal counseling to late-night phone calls, we are there for them, helping them, supporting them, and serving them right up to the moment they tell us they are leaving the church. Right up to the moment they tell us God is leading them to leave our church or they say they will no longer be supporting our ministry.

At that point, the reasons for them leaving are irrelevant to us. It just doesn't matter. All we know is we feel like we have invested our life in someone with little, if any, appreciation for what we have done, and it hurts. Especially for those who have become your close friends.

It hurts! It hurts! It hurts!

After all, we're the one who married their children and buried their family members, laughed with them, cried with them, served them, and prayed for them. Many who are reading this book know exactly what I'm talking about. It makes us feel like asking, "What's the point? Was it all for nothing?" When we're hurt badly enough, it makes us hesitate to invest again – especially after our last investment bottomed out and we lost everything.

Is it right or wrong to feel this way? Good question. All I know for sure is that it happens, and it hurts. I'm sure if you have been in ministry for very long, you have probably experienced this, and you know it hurts. You probably also know about the temptation to no longer invest. But it's good to learn what is written in *The Chronicles of Leroy*: "Pastors are in the people business because people last forever!"

I want bring encouragement to continue to invest in people's lives because our investment will produce dividends either in this life or the eternal life to come. I have a few investment tips to be considered.

First, we must settle in our heart that they are not our sheep. *They are not our sheep.* They belong to the Lord. The Lord is the one who bought and paid for them with His blood. If those sheep wander away from our sheepfold and end up somewhere else where they are fed and nourished, that's a good thing. After all, we want the Lord's sheep to be strong and healthy.

I believe one of the reasons we struggle with the loss of sheep is due to our ownership mentality. We hang on too tight to our investment, sometimes to the point of control and manipulation because we demand a return. My first investment tip is to remember they're not our sheep. We may not hurt any less, but it will help us to let go.

My second investment tip is for us to understand our effort will produce a return in the long run. What we have sown into their lives will produce fruit that glorifies God on earth and will produce a reward for us in heaven. Their salvations are stars in our crown. We brought repentance and sanctification into their lives, and this will produce a return as they live out their lives. The love, peace, joy, hope, and faith they experience because of our investment will yield returns in their life now and throughout eternity. One day, though we may not see it, they will produce fruit from the seeds we have sown.

If we have taught them to follow the leading of the Holy Spirit, how to discern God's will, and be guided by His word, then that is exactly what they are doing, so we help them pack their bags. Basically, we're the reason they are following the leadership ;of the Holy Spirit in leaving our church.

My investment tip is this. Our investment will produce a return both in this life and in our eternal reward to come. Remember this when you're helping them pack their bags;

although this is a bittersweet part of ministry and it may be the closing of our part in their story, we are storing up treasure in heaven for ourselves and bringing glory to God on earth.

Many times, I've had people leave who I thought would stay forever, and it always hurts. My investment was great in their lives, and I never expected them to leave. Today, I can testify of how God uses those people to bring Him glory with their lives. Some have even started churches and ministries or support others. I can testify of so many, still to this day, which have pursued God's call on their lives, following His Spirit. I know this is true because many have contacted me about how powerfully the ministries of our church and me as their pastor impacted their lives during the season they were here. They've told me how their lives were transformed and blessed and how the Lord brought restoration in their marriages, family and personal lives. How could I not be thankful for helping them pack their bags?

My third tip for those who have invested into people's lives is: don't hang on - let go! We have the tendency to want to hang on to sheep that need to be let go. It's wise to understand if they have made up their minds to leave our church or ministry, nothing we say or do is going to make them stay. Believe me, we can't convince them, and neither can we force them or guilt them into it. We must let them go.

In fact, the longer we try to hang on, the more

destructive things can become for us and the church or ministry. When we won't let go, they often begin to criticize us and will ultimately leave anyway. Many times, they take others with them. Therefore, holding on can cause greater losses.

It's wise to understand some people leave because God is leading them out, but sometimes the Lord is removing them for the sake of unity, and we have to let them go. Their slander and criticism of us, the church or other members prompted the Holy Spirit to remove them. We must accept what the Holy Spirit is doing in removing people who refuse to repent and have become a source of division and strife. Again, let them go. My experience with this has been that a great peace and unity will come among those who stay. Also, there will be a greater sense of the presence of the Lord in the meetings.

There are some sheep that wander off due to sin issues or deceptions in their lives. Our job, in this case, is to go after them.

Galatians 6:1 "Brethren, if a man is overtaken in any trespass, you who are spiritual restore such a one in a spirit of gentleness, considering yourself lest you be tempted." NKJV

It's interesting that Jesus went after his investment into Peter, but he let go of His investment in Judas.

Pastor Ed Herald, from Victory Church, said this about stewardship versus ownership.

Are we stewards of God's blessings or are we owners of His

blessings? Sounds like a simple question to answer, doesn't it? But anyone who refuses to answer too quickly may be surprised to find out they are often in the wrong seat when it comes to stewardship or ownership. You might be alarmed to realize you are sitting in the owner's seat most of the time. It's easy to do because we can easily confuse stewarding with owning. Are we stewards of God's blessings or are we owners?

This is a question that will undoubtedly help bring balance to our life and challenge us to look deep inside for the answer.

Some associate stewardship solely with financial issues, but that's not the case. Stewardship saturates every area of our life, not just our money. Stewardship involves our time, our talents, our treasures and our temple. In fact, everything in life is about stewardship, not about ownership. Everything is already His.

Psalms 24:1 "The earth is the Lord's, and all its fullness, the world and those who dwell therein." NKJV

The argument of who owns it is lost with this verse. This is critically important when we are dealing with challenges in our life. This is when we tend to take the seat of the owner. Ownership equals control. But not only does He own it all, we own nothing. In fact, when we die, we take nothing with us because it is not ours to take.

1 Timothy 6:6-7 "Now godliness with contentment is great gain. For we brought nothing into this world, and it is certain we can carry nothing out." NKJV

Job 1:20-21 "Then Job arose, tore his robe, and shaved his head; and he fell to the ground and worshiped. And he said: 'Naked I came from my mother's womb, and naked shall I return there. The Lord gave, and the Lord has taken away. Blessed be the name of the Lord'." NKJV

Could it be that Job said this because he knew it wasn't his, anyway? Why is this so important? The owner is the person that is responsible for the outcome not the steward. If we see things from the vantage point of a steward, we will be less stressed about the outcome of things. The owner carries the stress.

That's what Peter wrote in 1 Peter 5:6-7. "Therefore, humble yourselves under the mighty hand of God, that He may exalt you in due time, casting all your care upon Him, for He cares for you." NKJV

Some of you may be thinking, I'm not responsible for the outcome? No, a steward is responsible to God, and God is responsible for the outcome. When we steward the blessings, God gives increase. He's responsible.

1 Corinthians 3:6-9 "I planted the seed, Apollos watered it, but God has been making it grow. So, neither the one who plants nor the one who waters are anything, but only God, who makes things grow. The one who plants and the one who waters have one purpose, and they will each be rewarded according to their own labor. For we are co-workers in God's service; you are God's field, God's building." NKJV

Planting and watering were Paul and Apollo's role in the growth of the seed. If we assume the role of owner, then we are setting ourselves up to be accountable for the outcome. Isn't that what leaders do? No, we do our part, and the rest is up to God.

If you go to your job and don't think the business is going in the right direction, you don't sit at the boss's desk to do it your way. You go to your desk and trust that the boss is in charge and running things the right way.

Pastor Ed has such good advice from which we can learn. What have you decided? Will you be an owner or a steward? The boss is waiting to hear. My hope and prayer are that the Lord would call us good shepherds of His flock.

TEN
THEY CALL ME A VISIONARY
NAVIGATING THROUGH THE
CHALLENGES OF CASTING VISION

At the end of the TV series, *Lonesome Dove*, the reporter doing a story of the two famous Texas Rangers, Augustus McRae and Woodrow F. Call, said to Captain Call, people say you were men of vision. The response from Captain Call was yes, a hell of a vision!

Even though this was a fictional story, I hope that is said about me someday. I hope people say that I was a man of vision. A hell of a vision! Pastors and ministry leaders, we must be men and women of vision. A vision so powerful the gates of hell shall not prevail against it. A vision so challenging only faith can achieve it. A vision so compelling all those that hear it will run with it.

After defining our success and now having a solid strategy in place, it's time to step up as a visionary. The visionary is the one who casts the vision, making it known so those who hear it can run with it.

Habakkuk 2:2 "Then the Lord answered me and said: 'Write the vision and make it plain on tablets, that he may run who reads it'." NKJV

What is your vision? Have you written it down? Have you made it plain so those who read it can run with it? Have you cast the vision in such a way that the people God has placed around you are excited about it? Do they believe in it to the point they want to help you accomplish it? As you think about those questions, is your answer yes, no, or I hope so? The only right answer is yes, and if your answer is no or I hope so, it's time to turn things around.

Someone said vision without action is nothing more than a dream. Action without vision is just passing time but vision with action can change the world! Vision requires action. Actions set goals. A goal is a vision with a deadline. So, what's your vision and what goals are you setting to get there?

King David had a vision to build the temple and his son, Solomon, ran with it. So, I ask you, are there sons and daughters in your house running with your vision? I'm speaking of those you have poured in to and raised up to accomplish the vision, those who have your heart for the work of the ministry that God has called you. These are the sons and daughters of your house.

You are a visionary whether you know it or not. If the Lord has raised you up to pastor or lead a ministry, you are the visionary. Now it's up to you to determine what kind of visionary you will be.

Habakkuk 2:1-3 "I will stand my watch and set myself

on the rampart and watch to see what He will say to me, and what I will answer when I am corrected. Then the Lord answered me and said: 'Write the vision and make it plain on tablets, that he may run who reads it. For the vision is yet for an appointed time; but at the end it will speak, and it will not lie. Though it tarries, wait for it; because it will surely come, it will not tarry'." NKJV

I love this passage because it gives me instructions for how I can receive the Lord's vision for my life and ministry. Habakkuk says I will stand my watch and set myself on the rampart and watch to see what He will say to me and what I will answer when I'm corrected. We all want to know God's vision for our life and ministry. The way we know His vision is by hearing His voice, so we posture ourselves in such a way that we are watching, listening, and ready to receive, even if it means correction.

Many leaders say I want to hear God's voice for my ministry, but I don't want to receive any correction. They say I don't want to change the way I'm doing things, the way I am thinking, or the way I'm acting. Habakkuk declares what I will answer when I'm corrected. Many times, we don't have the right answer when we are corrected. We don't have the answer God is looking for and the wrong answer can impact those destinations God has for our ministry.

The answer God is looking for is, yes, Lord! When the Lord is trying to bring correction in our life, the answer he is looking for is always "Yes, Lord!" We can't say, "No, Lord." We can say "no", but we can't say "No, Lord" because the word Lord carries the understanding of Lordship. The Lord is either Lord of all or not at all.

We tend to want to hold onto things that are destructive in our ministry such as bad decisions, bad leadership skills, bad attitudes and bad thinking. These things rob us of God's blessing and the success in ministry that He has for us to achieve.

Obstinance has a voice. We can hear that voice so clearly at times. The Holy Spirit also has a voice. We can discern His voice if we will let go of our obstinance to the Lord's correction. We must allow the voice of the Spirit to overrule the voice of obstinance. I want to hear the Lord's correction so I can reach the destination of God's vision for the ministry He has called me to. My responsibility is to posture myself in such a way that I can hear His voice, even if it's the voice of correction.

Habakkuk describes what posturing looks like as he prepares to receive God's vision. The first thing he says is "*I will stand my watch.*" We need to be in the right place to receive God's vision. We can never expect the world to give us direction for God's vision. We won't receive God's vision for our life or ministry sitting around hoping the Lord drops His vision in our lap. We're not going to receive God's vision for our life by hanging out with the wrong people, the ones that are constantly draining us of our faith. It is best if we disassociate from those who are full of doubt and unbelief. My advice is to associate with men and women of faith. We're not going to receive God's vision for our life if we're not in the place where He wants to share

His vision with us. It's time to stand watch. It is time to be in the place that God wants us so we can receive His vision.

Secondly, Habakkuk says, "*I will set myself upon the rampart.*" The rampart is a defendable place. That Hebrew word can be translated as "a fortress, stronghold, and a tower." If we are seeking God's vision for our life, we should start in a place of advantage over the enemy. Begin when you are spiritually and mentally healthy. Don't struggle through trying to seek the Lord's vision when you are beat up, worn-out, depressed, overwhelmed and defeated. In order to be in a good place to receive, be prepared mentally and spiritually before seeking the Lord for His vision.

Now, we're on a rampart. We have our advantage over the enemy, we're standing our watch and we're at the place where we need to be in order to receive God's vision and correction.

Then He says, "*Watch to see what He would say to me.*" The phrase *watch to see* has a primitive root meaning "to lean forward, to peer into the distance, to look up." Therefore, in our posturing, we lean forward to observe and we peer into the distance. We look up. We put effort into our process of hearing. It is important to be intentional about receiving the Lord's vision.

Too often, leaders assume they know the Lord's vision for their lives. Many are not intentional about receiving the Lord's vision. Some lean on their education, the model of other pastors or they are looking but not watching. Others are hoping to see, but not intentionally seeking.

It's interesting that he uses the word *watch* to see what the Lord would say to me. Other translations say *I will wait to see* but most use the word watch to see. He was watching to see. This tells us that we can discover God's will by what we're seeing, not just hearing.

Sometimes we can get confused about what we're hearing when what we see Him doing is so obvious, we can determine God's will by it. Lord, do I take this job? Do I pursue this career? Or go in this direction? Because of the signs He reveals to us, His will becomes more obvious, especially when doors open or close and when things start to fall into place or fall apart. The direction we go becomes obvious by what we're seeing take place in our lives. Sometimes faith is built by what we see, not just by what we hear.

Elijah prayed for God to open his servant's eyes so that he could see the armies of heaven that were protecting him. That built up his faith. They suddenly see into the unseen world and all that God has done to defeat the enemies. He was watching to see what the Lord was saying. Sometimes God's vision is obvious by what we're seeing.

God has a vision for us to receive and we stand our watch. We set ourselves upon the rampart and we know what our answer will be when we are corrected, and we watch to see. God has a vision and it's our responsibility to posture ourselves in such a way that we can know it.

Habakkuk 2:2 "Then the Lord answered me and said 'Write the vision and make it plain on tablets, that he may run who reads it'." NKJV

Now we have the Lord's vision revealed to us and it's our responsibility to make it plain on tablets, so those who read it can run with it. First, I make sure God's vision for my life and ministry is clearly understood and written on the tablets of my own heart so I can run with it before I share it with others. Many leaders fail to reach God's destinations because the vision has not been clearly written on the tablets of their own heart. How can we reach His destinations if we don't know what those destinations are? If we have no vision for His destinations, how can we possibly see how to get there? Would we even want to? It's our responsibility to write the vision and make it plain, so we can run with it and inspire others to join us.

When the vision comes, the challenge of faith comes with it. It is impossible to take faith out of the equation because without faith it is impossible to please God.

Hebrews 11:6 "But without faith it is impossible to please Him, for he who comes to God must believe that He is, and that He is a rewarder of those who diligently seek Him." NKJV

It's important to remember what Jesus wanted his disciples to understand concerning the *significance of the loaves.*

Mark 6:41–52 "Jesus took the five loaves and two fish, looked up toward heaven, and blessed them. Then, breaking the loaves into pieces, He kept giving the bread to the disciples so they could distribute it to the people. He also divided the fish for everyone to share. They all ate as much as they wanted, and afterward, the disciples picked up twelve baskets of leftover bread and fish. A total of 5,000 men and their families were fed from those loaves! Immediately after this, Jesus insisted that His disciples get back into the boat and head across the lake to Bethsaida, while He sent the people home. After telling everyone good-bye, He went up into the hills by Himself to pray. Late that night, the disciples were in their boat in the middle of the lake, and Jesus was alone on land. He saw that they were in serious trouble, rowing hard and struggling against the wind and waves. About three o'clock in the morning Jesus came toward them, walking on the water. He intended to go past them, but when they saw Him walking on the water, they cried out in terror, thinking He was a ghost. They were all terrified when they saw Him. But Jesus spoke to them at once. 'Don't be afraid,' He said. 'Take courage! I am here!' Then He climbed into the boat, and the wind stopped. They were totally amazed, for they still didn't understand the significance of the miracle of the loaves. Their hearts were too hard to take it in." NLT

In this story Jesus has multiplied the fish and the loaves feeding 5,000 men and their families. Then He insisted that His disciples get back into the boat and head across the lake to Bethsaida. Later that night, the disciples were stuck in the middle of the lake battling the wind and the waves. Jesus saw that they were in trouble from the shore, rowing hard and struggling against the wind and waves. Now, Jesus walking on the water hears them cry out in terror. Jesus tells them to take courage and not to be afraid. He then climbs into the boat and the wind stops. The scripture says they were totally amazed for they still didn't understand the significance of the miracle of the loaves because their hearts were too hard to take it in.

What I love about this story is that Jesus sees them in the middle of the lake, struggling against the wind and the waves, giving us confidence that no matter what storm we're going through, He knows exactly where we are. He has the power to calm our storms and give us peace even if it is late at night and we feel he is a long way away. Yet like those early disciples, it is important for us to understand the significance of the miracle of the loaves.

What was the significance of the loaves? When we find our vision struggling against the wind and the waves, and our faith is being tested, it is in understanding the significance of the loaves that will bring us peace and confidence in God. The significance of the miracle of the loaves is in understanding nothing is impossible for God. No matter what we are facing, whether it's our need for provision, for a miracle or the calming of our storms, nothing is impossible for God.

Luke1:37 "For nothing is impossible with God." NLT

As we face the challenges of faith, may we always remember the significance of the loaves, so that we might be considered visionaries.

ELEVEN

THEY CALL ME A FAILURE
NAVIGATING THROUGH THE CHALLENGES OF FAILURE

For pastors and ministry leaders the devastation of failure can come in many forms. For some it may look like a moral failure. For others it could be the failure of a marriage. It could be a financial failure or a business failure or the failure of a church or ministry. If a person has been in ministry for any length of time, they know how often the sense of failure can come to mind. If a person has lived long enough, they have probably experienced some form of failure in one or more of these areas.

Navigating through failure will be one of the greatest challenges we face in ministry. Failure impacts every area of our life; not just personal well-being and mental health, but it impacts our marriage, family, finances, as well as our future. This chapter is dedicated to all the failures out there who have determined to move forward in life.

I will begin with the story of the rebellious donkey. Then

I will share the most important truth we need to know as we go through the challenges of failure. When we understand this one simple truth, we will be able to navigate through any challenge that failure may produce in our life.

There is a story from long ago about a stubborn and rebellious donkey. This old donkey was as stubborn and rebellious as they come. The old farmer who owned him tried and tried to keep him from busting through the fence to get to the neighbor's apple tree. The old farmer warned him that if he kept eating those apples, it was going to kill him. The stubborn old donkey refused to listen to his master and kept on trespassing on the neighbor's land to eat the apples. Well, one day he ate and ate and ate those forbidden apples until sure enough, they made him so sick that he died. His master had warned him this would happen, so he left that old donkey to the buzzards and the hot sun. After a few years, all that was left of the donkey was his sun-bleached bones, scattered on the ground.

The story does not end there, and I will finish it later. First, let me share the most important truth we need to know about failure. *Failure is not the end of the man whose God believes in him,* even if he is as stubborn and rebellious as the old donkey in our story. Even if he makes decisions that lead to his destruction; even if that person has crossed the boundary lines and gorged on forbidden fruit. Their failure is not the end of them or God's calling upon their life, nor does it put a period on their future in ministry.

Failure is not the end of the man or woman whose God

believes in them. This was true of King David who had
Uriah killed so he could take Bathsheba, Uriah's wife, to be
his own wife. King David was a miserable failure but went
on to be one of the greatest kings spoken about in the Bible.
He was identified by God as a man after God's own heart.
King David defeated enemies of God and fulfilled God's
purpose for his life because failure is not the end of the man
whose God believes in him.

This is true for Peter in the New Testament. He denied
Christ three times. Let's not forget the Apostle Paul who
persecuted of the early church. Or how about Jonah? We
find him running from God and his calling. Yet God
restored him to his purpose of reaching Nineveh. Mary
Magdalene was certainly identified as a failure by her
community but became mightily used in service to our
Lord. Samson is an example of a person controlled by his
lustful desires but was used by God at the end of his life.

Judges 15:14-17 "When he came to Lehi, the Philistines
came shouting against him. Then the Spirit of the LORD
came mightily upon him; and the ropes that were on his
arms became like flax that is burned with fire, and his
bonds broke loose from his hands. He found a fresh
jawbone of a donkey, reached out his hand and took it, and
killed a thousand men with it. Then Samson said: "With the
jawbone of a donkey, Heaps upon heaps, With the jawbone
of a donkey I have slain a thousand men!" And so it was,
when he had finished speaking, that he threw the jawbone
from his hand, and called that place Ramath Lehi." NKJV

Samson started out as a mighty warrior whose ability

from God helped him to defeat thousands of God's enemies time after time in the most unusual ways. Samson said, "With the jawbone of a donkey, heaps upon heaps, with the jawbone of a donkey I have slain a thousand men!" Samson was later deceived by Delilah and captured by his enemies, blinded and then brought before the enemies of God to be mocked and ridiculed.

Judges 16:21 -30 "Then the Philistines took him and put out his eyes and brought him down to Gaza. They bound him with bronze fetters, and he became a grinder in the prison. However, the hair of his head began to grow again after it had been shaven. Now the lords of the Philistines gathered together to offer a great sacrifice to Dagon their god, and to rejoice. And they said: 'Our god has delivered into our hands Samson our enemy!' When the people saw him, they praised their god; for they said, 'Our god has delivered into our hands our enemy, the destroyer of our land, and the one who multiplied our dead.' So it happened, when their hearts were merry, that they said, 'Call for Samson that he may perform for us.' So, they called for Samson from the prison, and he performed for them. And they stationed him between the pillars. Then Samson said to the lad who held him by the hand, 'Let me feel the pillars which support the temple, so that I can lean on them.' Now the temple was full of men and women. All the lords of the Philistines were there—about three thousand men and women on the roof watching while Samson performed. Then Samson called to the Lord, saying, 'O Lord God, remember me, I pray! Strengthen me, I pray, just this once, O God that I may with one blow take vengeance on the Philistines for my two eyes!' And Samson took hold of the two middle pillars which supported the temple, and he braced himself against them, one on his right and the other on his left. Then Samson said, 'Let me die with the Philistines!' And he pushed with all his might, and the temple fell on the lords and all the people who were in it. So, the dead that he killed at his death were more than he had killed in his life." NKJV

Samson, after his failure, defeated more of God's enemies at his death than he did during his life. Failure is not the end of the man whose God believes in him! This was true for Samson, King David, the apostle Peter, the apostle Paul, Mary Magdalene and so many others throughout the Bible. This is also true for us.

Before I go on let me continue the story about the rebellious, stubborn donkey. Although it's a fictional story and not scriptural, I can't help but imagine that one day a man came along named Samson, picked up the jawbone of that donkey, and used it to slay a thousand of God's enemies. You see, failure is not the end of a donkey whose God believes in him, even if that stubborn donkey looks like you or me.

Like Samson, Peter, David, Mary and Paul we all have chapters in our lives that we wish we could delete or at the very least do over. I know I have those chapters in my life, chapters of poor decisions and failures. They have a way of hurting the people we love the most and robbing us of any hope for our future. I know what it feels like to look back on a chapter of my life and wish it had never been written. But like those men and women written about in the Lord's book for all to read, our choice is to get stuck in that chapter and burdened down by guilt and self-condemnation or let those chapters become our testimony of God's grace, mercy and power to restore for all to read. And may our choice be to move forward into God's purpose and destiny for our lives and ministry.

To those of us reading this who have suffered a failure of any kind in our life, lay hold of the fact that God sends our sins as far as the east is from west and chooses to remember them no more. His grace abounds toward us and He has never stopped loving us. Also, lay hold of the truth that nothing can separate us from His love. Not even our failure.

The most important thing to establish in our hearts is that God believes in us. Our God is the God of restoration, the God of second chances. It is so important to know and understand God alone has the power to restore us and will restore us because He believes in us. Trust Him and lay down your life on His altar. It's not easy. Restoration is the toughest challenge we will ever experience. The hardest part of that challenge is to remember the Lord believes in us and wants to restore us. It's equally as difficult to begin to believe in yourself again.

I pray we begin to see things from God's perspective. Just as God knew what would take place later in David's life when He chose him to be king and what would take place when He chose Peter to be His disciple, the Lord knew what would take place in our life and yet He still chose us. He chose us because He believes in us and He desires for us to believe in ourselves.

The Lord believes in us, or He would not have dialed up our number. I pray we remember this as we start our journey of restoration. Remember it when doubt and unbelief fill our hearts, and when we hear accusations and rumors. When the accuser of the brethren puts fear in our heart or the schemes and tactics of the enemy are overwhelming, this is our reminder that the Lord believes in us. Failure is not the end of the man whose God believes in him.

As I conclude this chapter, let's touch on what restoration requires, hoping anyone who has experienced moral failure will have an understanding of what is required for their restoration in ministry.

Restoration begins with repentance and acknowledging the brokenness that produced the sin. Afterward comes confessing and turning away from that sin. The Lord is very aware of what produces sin in our lives but sadly we often fail to see the real problem. Our brokenness, the broken issues of our heart, is the real problem. We have to acknowledge it and allow Jesus to heal it if we ever hope to see true restoration take place. Those who refuse to address and deal with the issue of brokenness are on the devil's timeline for future failure.

Repentance is defined by changing the way we think and the actions we take. We must ask ourselves why we think the way we do and take the actions we take. Often, the way we act and think results from the broken issues of our life. Those things must be examined, identified and set on a course for healing which I will address later in this chapter.

For restoration to occur we face the challenge of building trust again, whether that is from your spouse, family, or people who felt betrayed by our actions. Building trust takes time. It is not something we can expect just because we repented. Trust is not something we can demand from other people just because we've resolved to turn our lives around. Trust takes time and effort until earned and proven. If people don't trust us, they won't follow us. We build trust once again by the way we live a life of integrity before the Lord. The fruit of repentance is the evidence needed to earn trust.

Psalm18:25 "To the faithful you show yourself faithful; to those with integrity you show integrity." NLT

As we walk in integrity before the Lord, remember God is on our side helping us to prove we can be trusted. It is God who restores us after failure. We cannot do it by our own efforts. We must trust Him for restoration. Please don't try to force it; but rather trust God's timing and process for restoration. We only push back God's timetable if we try to force it. We must trust God until God shows people they can trust us again. As it is written in *The Chronicles of Leroy*, "The greatest challenge of Christianity is not faith, but trust, because trust is the proof of faith."

After a failure in ministry, we face the challenge of humility, the challenge of walking in humility throughout the process of restoration. Humility in God's eyes looks like taking responsibility for our actions. Pride casts blame. Humility accepts responsibility. Pride looks outward, humility looks inward.

It is a humbling thing to stand before people and confess our sin, weakness, and brokenness, when our whole life has been about setting the example for others to follow. It is one thing to know we're a miserable failure it's another thing to acknowledge it to others. And believe me I know exactly what this feels like. But aren't we all just miserable failures that are trusting in the grace, mercy and righteousness of Christ? King David humbled himself after his failure, confessed his sin, and accepted responsibility for his actions. He did not hide his sin or hide from people, he truly accepted the fact that he failed God, other people, and failed himself. Being humble and totally dependent upon God's grace is the first step toward the healing of our brokenness. If we want to be whole, we must be honest with ourselves, other people, and the Lord.

James 4:6 "But He gives more grace. Therefore, He says, 'God resists the proud, but gives grace to the humble'."

It is the grace of God - His kindness and favor upon our lives - that we desperately need for restoration to take place. When there is pride, there only comes destruction. Only God can restore us to His fullness after failure. It is when we have His embrace, because of our humility, that He begins the process of restoration. If we refuse to admit fault, or refuse to look at our own brokenness, it reeks of pride, and God's work of restoration is put on hold.

Our own pride is often hard to discern. We tend to spot

it in others, but not in ourselves. Others can see it in us, but we are blind to it. This is why it is such a challenge. Our own pride can shield us from the truth. The challenge is humility and accepting responsibility for our actions.

Lastly, there is the challenge of allowing God to heal the brokenness in our life. Brokenness can be the root cause of so many failures in our lives, but the ministry of Jesus is our pathway to healing.

Jesus said in Luke 4:18-19, "The Spirit of the Lord is upon me, because He hath anointed me to preach the gospel to the poor; he hath sent me to heal the brokenhearted, to preach deliverance to the captives, and recovering of sight to the blind, to set at liberty them that are bruised, to preach the acceptable year of the Lord." KJV

Jesus came to give us everything we need to experience a life in Christ. We understand the ministry of Jesus is the Gospel message, the year of jubilee, but the ministry of Jesus is also about the opening of our blind eyes, the healing of our broken heartedness, liberty from those things that hold us captive, and freedom from the bruises of life. The ministry of Jesus is our pathway to our healing, freedom, and His blessing upon our lives and ministries.

Let me break this passage down into four revelations of the ministry of Jesus.

First, the ministry of Jesus is to heal the brokenhearted. He wants to heal our broken heart and the things in life that break our heart. These things could be tragedies, disappointments, unfulfilled expectations, hurtful relationships, and betrayals. Life has a way of breaking our heart. But because of Jesus, we do not have to live with a broken heart.

The word *broken* in the Greek is *suntribo*. It means "to crush completely, to shatter, to tread down, travel upon, to break into pieces, to smash."

The tragedies, disappointments, the unfulfilled expectations and betrayals have a way of breaking our heart, shattering it and grinding it down to pieces. People have a way of treading upon it and crushing it. There are things that happen in life that break our heart and there are things that people do to us that break our heart.

We understand that the heart is the seat of our emotions. I believe this is why so many people have emotional breakdowns and go through times of emotional instability. If that is you, Jesus is your pathway to freedom. He can heal your broken heart. Just ask Him and allow Him to heal you. Healing starts by asking and it is received by believing.

The ministry of Jesus is all about healing the broken-hearted. I pray we receive the revelation of this ministry of Jesus.

Psalm 147:3 "He heals the brokenhearted and bandages their wounds." NLT

While reading this, if the Holy Spirit has been bringing any brokenness to the surface, it is for a reason. Do not push something down that the Holy Spirit is bringing up. Do not try to hide what the Holy Spirit is exposing. Freedom comes by receiving and believing.

Secondly, Jesus also brings deliverance to the captives. The ministry of Jesus is about deliverance or setting free those who are in bondage or held captive by demonic control. We know Jesus is our deliverer. That word, *captive*, literally means "a prisoner of war," a P.O.W.

Many in the body of Christ are held captive. Some are held captive by sin and some by demonic control. These people are stuck in a cage in some area of their life. They believe they have no way out. They just need to understand that Jesus is their pathway to freedom. He has come to bring deliverance to the captives.

Acts 10:38 "And you know that God anointed Jesus of Nazareth with the Holy Spirit and with power. Then Jesus went around doing good and healing all who were oppressed by the devil." NKJV

Jesus is our way out, just do not give up. If we're tempted to give up, press forward and don't stop because deliverance is coming. I say this under the unction of the Holy Spirit. Don't give up! Give in! Give in and allow the power of the Lord Jesus Christ to set you free. Give in to the Holy Spirit to rule and reign in your life. Give in and shut every door that gives the enemy access into your life. So, give in. Don't give up.

Thirdly, the ministry of Jesus is to give sight to the blind. This relates to the power of Jesus to open blind eyes in the natural, but it also relates to spiritual blindness, those who can't see the truth. They are the ones that can't see who Jesus is or understand why He came.

It relates to Jesus helping us see what we cannot see, the things that keep us from the abundant life Jesus came to give us, according to the Gospel of John 10:10. The Lord wants to reveal the pride issues in our life that have us blinded to what He wants us to see. Jesus came to heal the brokenhearted and set the captives free. Jesus, open our blind eyes and set at liberty those that are bruised.

Lastly, the ministry of Jesus is to set at liberty those that are bruised.

It's interesting to me that the ministry of Jesus is to set at liberty those that are bruised. That phrase, *set at liberty* in the Greek, means "to release from imprisonment". Jesus is our 'get out of jail' free card. We do not have to stay in prison by the bruises of life or by those things in life that bruise our soul or our mental well-being. This can bruise how we think and feel about ourselves and others in our life. The bruises of life can affect us mentally and are very destructive.

I have a friend who recently told me that he hated people. He just hates people. Imagine living out our life hating everyone. He is in a spiritual prison because of the bruises of his life. I cannot talk him out of hating people, but I can help him understand the ministry of Jesus and give him a get out of jail free card.

The King James Version uses the word *bruise*. A bruise is an inward bleeding. A bruise does not hurt unless you touch it. We're all familiar with bruises caused by a bumping into something or accident of some kind. When we look at it, we can see it. It is black and blue, but it really doesn't hurt unless we touch it. Well, the devil knows how to touch it and can cause pain and sorrow in our lives. People also know how to touch it, causing pain and sorrow in our lives. People get imprisoned by these bruises of life.

It can relate to our memories, or those things stored up in our memory banks. That is why we can just be doing well emotionally and mentally as Christians until the devil touches those bruises. We hear the jail door slammed shut and the handcuffs click around our wrists. The ministry of Jesus is to get us out of the prison of our bruises.

This is our destination. It is up to us to begin the journey; to start the pathway to freedom and allow Jesus to set us free from the bruises of life. It is as simple as asking the Holy Spirit to bring up any memories that the Lord wants to heal and then taking those memories one by one through the process of asking the Lord to heal that memory. To heal that memory from all that hurts all the pain all the sorrow all the grief and all the guilt associated with that memory. And then asking the Holy Spirit to give us a holy forgetfulness and lastly declaring that this memory is now healed by the power of God and Satan no longer has power over that memory any longer. I have done this many times with groups of people and it's amazing how the Holy Spirit brings up hurtful memories. It's also amazing to watch how powerful prayer and declaration brings healing and deliverance from those memories. I challenge you to go through this process and then take others through it. Everyone needs to experience freedom from life's bruises.

I want to go back for a moment speaking about the ministry of Jesus to open our blind eyes. Sometimes the pathway to freedom is simply us. The only thing holding us back from the abundant life Jesus came to give us is ourselves. The only thing keeping us and our ministry from the restoration God has for us is us. We are not blind because we want to be blind; we are blind because we refuse to see what Jesus wants us to see.

Sometimes our pathway to freedom is within us, seeing what God wants us to see. One of the most destructive things operating in the life of a believer is what I call blinding pride. When our pride blinds us, we can't see, and we need the Lord to open our blind eyes.

James 4:6 "But he gives more grace. Therefore, He says: 'God resists the proud, but gives grace to the humble'." NKJV

I interpret this to mean that God will take a battle stance against the proud. God resists the proud. The Greek word for *pride* in this passage means "to show oneself above others, an overwhelming estimate of one's means or merits, despising others or even treating them with contempt or being haughty."

I have always defined pride as being unteachable, unchangeable, and unreasonable. We just cannot reason with these kinds of people. They only see their own viewpoint and refuse to change. They will not listen; they think they know it all and refuse to change or be teachable. That is my definition of pride. That's why I call it blinding pride. They are blind to the real problem, which is themselves. However, the last thing these kinds of people would do is to take ownership or blame.

Proverbs 16:18 "Pride goes before destruction, and haughtiness before a fall." NLT

This proverb makes it clear what is on the horizon of pride's life. The good news is, God resists the proud but gives grace to the humble. Grace which offers joy, pleasure, delight, loveliness, good will, and loving-kindness paints the picture of God's favor. One is a battle stance against and the other and is an embrace of favor.

Blinding pride is the pride we cannot see that operates in our lives that cause us most of our problems. I think we can all relate to having blinding pride operating at some point in our Christian walk. I know that there were times in my life where I just could not see that the real problem was me, and I found myself blaming everyone but myself. Pride casts blame and never accepts responsibility for its actions.

When we are struggling with pride issues that are causing us to blame everyone but ourselves, we need a Jimmy Buffett revelation. The song *Margaritaville* tells the story of a guy wasting away while looking for his lost shaker of salt and trying to figure out who was to blame for his condition. He starts out by saying that some people say there's a woman to blame but he knew it wasn't her fault. As the song continues, he is strumming his six-string guitar while continuing to look for his lost shaker of salt then he begins to think it could be his fault. After he stepped on a pop top then blew out his flip-flop while still looking for his lost shaker of salt, he finally realized it was his own darn fault.

Jimmy finally came to the revelation that the problems

in his life were his fault. The pride in his life was blinding him to the truth until he finally accepted responsibility. Though I used this example in jest, we all need that Jimmy Buffett revelation when our blinding pride is causing us problems.

The greatest need in our lives is the ministry of Jesus! This is our pathway to freedom and wholeness so that restoration can come to our lives and ministry. Have you received His entire ministry since you believed? May they never call us a failure again!

TWELVE
THEY CALL ME A WARRIOR
NAVIGATING THROUGH THE DIFFICULT
SEASONS OF MINISTRY

Perhaps I should have titled this chapter "Difficult Seasons" or "Battle Scars".

Either title works, because as warriors, we have our battle scars, and all go through difficult seasons of ministry. As we'll learn from my pastor friends who share their stories of challenging times later in this chapter, we should understand that it's just a season. Difficult seasons come and go.

Some may be reading this chapter on a Monday morning after pouring our heart into a Sunday sermon delivered to a sparse, apathetic audience. The disappointment lingers, and we're left questioning the worth of our efforts, battling the heavy sense that it might all be in vain. Maybe we should give up.

I have two things to say. The first is welcome to the ministry, and the second is we are giving up too soon.

Please don't give up. We have all gone through what you're going through, and we have all felt the same thing so just hold tight and look toward the bigger picture.

An article from Barna titled *New Data Shows Hopeful Increase in Pastors' Confidence & Satisfaction* dated March 6, 2024 states 33% of pastors have considered leaving full-time ministry. Think about what would happen to the church if 33% of the pastors quit. What happens to our culture and society if 33% of pastors quit?

Look at the bigger picture. I will to do my best to build up our faith because after all, isn't giving up is a faith issue? I believe a breakthrough in ministry is just on the other side of the testing of our faith. That may be something we don't want to hear; however, it is the absolute truth.

2 Samuel 5:20 "so David went to Baal Perazim, and David defeated them there; and he said, 'The Lord has broken through my enemies before me, like a breakthrough of water.' Therefore, he called the name of that place Baal Perazim." NKJV

King David kept fighting and breakthrough came. We need to keep on fighting. Just like the Apostle Paul advised after being beaten, stoned, shipwrecked, bitten by a snake and imprisoned: stay the course.

Many of us have been stoned by those we have given our lives to. We have been shipwrecked in our faith and no doubt snake bitten by constant demonic attack. Maybe some have even been imprisoned by our doubt-filled thought life. My encouragement is to stay the course; don't give up. If pastoral ministry was easy, everyone would do it.

Instead of giving up, give in to Him and find a place of resting in the Lord. As we realize we can't make it happen, we can begin to rest and trust the Lord for His timing and process for our success. Go back and review your definition of success. Remember, it is God's definition for our success and no one else's. We must understand that our success is up to Him and not us alone.

Make an acrostic for REST. As an example, this is the one I use.

R: Remember the great things God has done in my life and ministry.

E: Eat from His Word so I will be strengthened.

S: Start each day in His presence, praising Him so I experience refreshing, etc.

T: Trust Him with all my heart and lean not on my own understanding.

Come up with your own acrostic for REST, it will mean more to you.

Victory in the midst of the battle comes by resting in the Lord. Moses was sitting down on the rock when victory came over the enemy.

Exodus 17:11-13 "And so it was, when noses held up his hand, that Israel prevailed; and when he let down his hand, Amalek prevailed. But Moses' hands became heavy; so, they took a stone and put it under him, and he sat on it. And Aaron and Hur supported his hands, one on one side, and the other on the other side; and his hands were steady until the going down of the sun. So, Joshua defeated Amalek and his people with the edge of the sword." NKJV

Our rock to rest upon is Christ Jesus. Yes, Moses needed help to hold up his tired arms and so do we from those God sends to support us. This reminds us to let the people God sends to us know when we are tired and ready to give up. Then they can lift us up in prayer and support.

Remember, if God did not believe in us, he would not have dialed up our number and called us to do what He has put in our hearts to do. Don't hang up, hang on. The one thing pastors know about is fighting the fight and not hanging up.

I am reminded of the story of a missionary I once knew named Sam Sasser. He was a missionary to the Solomon Islands. Sam had many difficulties and adversities in his life and ministry. He endured persecution, physical attacks, coral poisoning and a shipwreck.

I remember Sam telling a group of pastors the story of when he most felt like giving up. He was in the Solomon Islands doing mission work and had not seen his wife in over a year because she was back in the States. He was having little, if any, success in reaching the people there in the islands. He brought a local prostitute to the Lord who just happened to be the favorite prostitute of one of the local sea captains. When the sea captain returned from sea to discover she was now a Christian due to Sam's influence, the sea captain found Sam and beat him severely. Two local islanders were watching and intervened and then beat the sea captain until he was unconscious. At that point, Sam stopped the two islanders and cared for the sea captain, tending to his wounds. He eventually was able to lead that sea captain to the Lord.

Later, upon being arrested by the local authorities for sharing his faith, Sam was put in an 8 X10 metal shed that was being used as a jail. The worst part was there was a dead nine-year-old boy inside the shed. Sam was finally let out and released after three days in that hot, humid shed filled with the smell of death.

After his release, he started walking to the house where he was staying on the far side of the island. Sam told us the entire time he was walking he was thinking about how he was ready to give up and go home. As he walked, a man in an old car pulled alongside him. The man asked Sam if he wanted a ride, and Sam took him up on the offer.

As they drove, the man asked him if he had heard about what was happening. Sam replied that he didn't know. Astonished the man explained that they were sending men to the moon and that it would be broadcast on the radio, referring to Apollo 11. Sam said this bit of good news from home made him anxious to get to where he was staying so he could listen to the radio. When he arrived home, he quickly took a spool of wire and wrapped it around a tree serving as the antenna for his radio.

He finally got everything hooked up at the very moment that the lunar lander was separating from Apollo 11 to descent to the surface of the moon. It was at the very point where the astronaut was communicating to Cape Canaveral and he heard the voice of the astronaut as they were disengaging and beginning their descent say these words, "Canaveral we have committed."

At that very moment, Sam heard the Holy Spirit ask him the question, "Are you committed?" Sam went on to have a tremendous impact on the Solomon Islands with the gospel of Jesus Christ. Those words still ring in my ear when I'm going through the trials and tribulations of ministry: are you committed?

I asked some pastor friends of mine to tell their stories of the most difficult seasons of their ministries and how they navigated through those seasons and what they learned. I also asked these pastors to share what kept them hanging on when they felt like giving up.

Here are their answers:

Olen Griffing, Senior Pastor, Shady Grove Church, Grand Prairie, TX

My most difficult season was when the deacons in the church I was pastoring tried their best to get me voted out, but it failed. Then the church building was totally destroyed by arson. Then the Dallas Baptist Association disfellowshipped me and our church. This all happened in the first 15 months that I was pastor. It was knowing that God had called me to this ministry, therefore, I wasn't giving up.

Kerry Kirkwood, Senior Pastor, Trinity Fellowship, Tyler, Texas

There becomes a point of no return when the disappointments and the betrayals have less effect on you and you know the Holy Spirit leading you is more defining than what someone else has said, to become obsessed with the presence of God pushes me past trying to build a ministry. For me there was no plan B, like I will try this and if it doesn't work, I can go back to my business life.

The process I take myself through is turning my affections towards the Lord and remembering the lions and the bears I conquered, encouraging myself in the Lord. Also reminding myself of all those I have to lead, including my family, motivates me to not give up, as they depend upon me to be strong.

Ed Harold, Senior Pastor, Victory Church, Bloomington, IL

The past few years have been the most challenging of my entire 28 years in ministry. From my oldest son becoming angry at me and leaving the family. I haven't seen him since. The trials of Covid, racial tension, the 2020 election. That was fun. Then in 2022, we experienced a fire at our church that destroyed everything. I mean everything. I have a message I have prepared called "10 Totes." That's what we took out to be salvaged. After 28 years of ministry and now only 10 totes to show for it, it took my counselor to remind me that "which was done still remains." WOW. Another sermon title.

Bonus, in March of the same year as our fire, we had an uprising in leadership (another fire) that went completely out of control leading the church to its first ever split. We tried for 10 months to avoid what became evident that it had to be. Over 55 members left the church in the middle of a church rebuild project. Mostly leadership and strong supporters. As we were just getting some footing, and if all that wasn't enough, we received a call from the Sheriff's office late one evening in February 2023, that they were called to check on reports of suspicious activity at the church building site. Turns out that it was way more than suspicious activity.

A 20-year-old man was taken to the property then shot and killed. Now a murder on the land we dedicated to God. Not the way I wanted to start the year, nor the publicity we asked for, and with those that left the church, the cursing words were flying.

As Beth and I were once again driving to church with racing uncertainty, I looked at her and said, "How are we going to deal with all of this?" I don't recall her response to be truthful, I was in a catatonic state at the time. Since then, I have spent a lot of time reflecting on all that has happened. Something occurred to me … I'm still standing. Then the picture of a tree came to mind.

On researching this, I found this article that I feel perfectly illustrates my journey over the past few years. It's from the *Entrepreneurial Learning Initiative* website. "Strong Winds Strong Roots: What Trees Teach Us About Life." To conclude this month's Top of Mind newsletter, we visited an ecological experiment set in a desert called the bio-dome. In it are, seemingly, the perfect conditions for growing fruits, vegetables, and trees, and it was a place where humans could live happily for months at a time. When the trees grew to a certain height, they would topple over. It baffled scientists until they realized they forgot to include the natural element of wind. Trees need wind to blow against them because it causes their root systems to grow deeper, which supports the tree as it grows taller. Watch an old, strong tree in the wind the next time it storms. It sways and bends with the wind, remaining in flow with the surrounding energy. While the wind, at times, has the power to upend a tree in the wind, one that has gone through many storms will probably withstand many more, for its roots are deep and strong. The metaphor here is that to grow deeply, we cannot hide in a dome; we must live in the world around.

This was me for sure. For so long, I lived in the relative safety of self-inflicted inferiority. I had some fruit and produce from the labor that I had done in ministry, but not what God saw in me. As the winds blew against me, my family, and the church, something happened I didn't see coming. My roots grew. Each day that I got up and withstood the winds, there was something in my spirit that simply would not give up. It's like my roots knew that there was more to do, so they dug in. They reached deeper so the strength of the wind was matched by the depth of the roots. So, because of blowing the winds of the past few years, I grew stronger and taller. I'm 6'4 so I'm not looking for additional physical height. But in the spirit, I'm growing taller. My previous roots were enough to support where I was, but not where I was going/growing.

I've learned that my response to the wind matters more than the wind itself. It's much like the disciples in James 1:2 "My brethren, count it all joy when you fall into various trials, knowing that the testing of your faith produces patience. But let patience have its perfect work, that you may be perfect and complete, lacking nothing.

I'm certainly not asking for more wind in my life. I feel like we have been in a tornado alley these last few years. But at least now, I know how to respond to the wind so I can grow by it.

. . .

*Stephen McCoy, Senior Pastor, The Heights Church, Hillsboro,
TX*

*Psalm 92:12-15 "The righteous shall flourish like a palm tree,
He shall grow like a cedar in Lebanon. Those who are planted in
the house of the Lord shall flourish in the courts of our God. They
shall still bear fruit in old age; they shall be fresh and flourishing,
to declare that the Lord is upright; He is my rock, and there is no
unrighteousness in Him."*

*The way we were able to navigate through not becoming the
Senior Pastor, was to continue to sit at the feet of Jesus. Not my
will be done, but His will be done. We have been serving now at
The Heights Church for 38 years. There have been so many times
we wanted to leave because of offenses. Each time we would sit at
the feet of Jesus and listen. We refused to drink of the poison of
offense. We chose to repent and forgive. I want to be like Jesus.
One of the last things Jesus wanted to make sure we got when he
was hanging on the cross was forgiveness. He looked up to the
Father and said, "Father, forgive them for they know not what
they are doing." I encourage each of you, no matter what
disappointments or battles you're facing; always sit at the feet of
Jesus and listen.*

Psalm 46:10 "Be still and know that I am God."

*We live our lives by.W.W.P. Word, worship, and prayer. We
live a life of the Word! Psalm 119 says, "Great peace have they
which love thy law; and nothing shall offend them."*

We must put the word in us when we don't need it so it will be there when we do need it. When do we need it? We need it when we find ourselves in unexpected circumstances that could offend or disappoint us. Read and meditate in God's Word every day.

We live a life of worship! Psalm 71:8 "Let my mouth be filled with thy praise and with thy honor all day." We live a life of prayer!

I Thessalonians 16-18 "Rejoice always, pray without ceasing, in everything give thanks; for this is the will of God in Christ Jesus for you."

1 Corinthians 9:24 "Do you not know that those who run in a race all run, but one receives the prize? Run in such a way that you may obtain it. And everyone who competes for the prize is temperate in all things. Now they do it to obtain a perishable crown, but we for an imperishable crown. Therefore, I run this, not with uncertainty. Thus, I fight; not as one who beats the air. But I discipline my body and bring it into subjection, lest, when I have preached to others, I myself should become disqualified."

If we do these things, we will fulfill our God-given destinies and be able to say what Paul said.

2 Timothy 4:6 "For I am already being poured out as a drink offering, and the time of my departure is at hand. I have fought the good fight, I have finished the race, I have kept the faith. Finally, there is laid up for me the crown of righteousness, which the Lord, the righteous Judge, will give to me on that Day, and not to me only but also to all who have loved His appearing."

. . .

Wayne Lymden, Pastoral ministry 23 years

    The most difficult thing my wife and I had to go through in ministry was something that occurs in almost everybody's life. We had a business burn to the ground, and it wasn't that. We had a church split, and that wasn't it either. The loss of our son due to an overdose is what became our most difficult hardship. It shattered us and made us question everything we knew about God, Christ, and the Holy Spirit, trying to figure out what went wrong, what did we miss and could we have prevented it. We were overcome with guilt, emotional breakdown and sadness that wouldn't quit. All of our family, five boys and two girls, devastated by this surprising death to one who was so vibrant and contagious to the whole family. He was the one who tied us all together. We spoke almost daily with Jon and never suspected anything. Although he lived in a different state, he visited often. The greatest question was, "Is he going to heaven or not?"

    We thought about his commitment, baptism, youth group, church attendance, all the right things. God brought me to John 3:16-18. As I read that, this is the condemnation that they denied; they did not confess Jesus Christ, and it was here that I realized our son had never denied his faith in Jesus Christ. This all affected the church, and I don't know whether they thought we had sin in our life or were too broken to minister, but things were not the same. We made a huge mistake by not taking a sabbatical of at least three weeks. I jumped back into pastoral duties after only a week and my emotions were still very raw. We cried ourselves to sleep for quite some time. Our pastor told us, "He who loves deeply, grieves deeply." It was quite a while after Jon's death that God spoke to me and said that you can choose to live in the past and not be useful to Me or live in the present and serve Me with your whole heart. That is what made the difference.

Death has a very strong impact on people and the church. Many people do not know how to deal with it or process it. People have to be taught how to address someone who has lost a loved one, otherwise many times they blurt out words that can hurt, ostracize, and separate. Jon's death was a great eye opener to us and how we minister to other grieving families. Yes, before I forget, God did tell me something that brought such clarity and life to me when He said, "You know, son, "I lost a Son as well."" *What we learned is everybody grieves, but not all the same. Grief can't be rushed, nor should it be compared to someone else's experience to make people conform. You need to remove yourself from duties until you are receiving healing and able to talk more freely about your loved one's death. Rest in the wisdom and sovereignty of God. Trust the outcome to Him who knows all things and is perfect in all His ways. Get together with your leadership and be human. We're not invincible and people need to understand that. I hope this helps because the greatest help was a person who says, "I'm really sorry for your loss." They remained silent and held your hand.*

Kody Hughes, Senior Pastor, the Heights Church, Cleburne, TX

In every leader's life, one of the greatest challenges will be change. Change is inevitable. Everything that grows changes. You could say, "Everything that goes changes." If you are leading, that means you are going somewhere. Hopefully, as a leader people are following you. If not, you're just taking a walk. If you do have followers that means you are taking them somewhere and that will always involve change. I like to use the word "transition." It just feels more comfortable, either way, transition or change is a very healthy part of leadership. It's actually what people long for, they just don't know it.

Transition is the difficult place of not being where you used to be and not quite being where you want to be, and trust me, in leadership, you will find yourself there often. It's one of the most difficult, yet profitable places to be. So many great things happen in transition.

Let me explain. For a pregnant woman, excited about birthing a child, she will learn this word, "transition." In childbirth, transition is the place between heavy contractions and delivery. It's a place a woman's body goes to when the most painful, yet productive, moments are about to arrive. You see, transition is the place when the child goes through the squeeze and the mother goes through intense pain, pushing a baby into this new world. Most women decide in this moment that they no longer want to be pregnant and say, "I can't do this." Or they may even say to the man who helped get her there, "I hate you." The pain of transition is so intense that we are willing to abandon everything. What many don't realize is transition causes a great bond with the soon coming child. There's a deep, intimate connection happening when a mother and child go through transition. There are also some healthy things happening for the baby. It's in transition that all the fluid is being squeezed out of the lungs of the child being delivered. Without that fluid being squeezed out, that child would drown after being born.

The same is true with any leader that finds themselves in transition. It can be one of the most painful seasons in a leader's life. You may have been excited about what's ahead and couldn't wait until something new was birthed in your ministry or area of leadership, but when the time comes, we often change our mind because of how hard transition can be.

For me personally, transition has come in several ways and has happened several times. Though I despised it when I was younger, I get excited about it now. One of my first transitions as a leader came when my pastor, who was my father-in-law and best friend, suddenly died of cancer. Actually, he had battled cancer for several years but somehow, we think that great leaders will never die.

I had been serving as the executive pastor to one of the greatest pastors I had ever known. I also married his daughter, so we were extremely close. When transition happened suddenly, it was a bit overwhelming. The leadership of the church knew that one day I would pastor the church. That had been communicated to them by our pastor. That day just came sooner than expected and I found myself amid transition. What will happen to the church after losing a pastor they had followed for 33 years? Would they follow me like they followed him? I felt so unqualified and unprepared. My thought was, "God, please don't let me mess things up." There were many years of legacy that I was now responsible for stewarding. We had a large congregation and had recently moved into a new sanctuary. But now our senior pastor had passed away, and I found myself the senior leader. I didn't feel ready, but I realize now we probably never are. The entire city began to wonder, "What will happen to such a big church in transition?" Fortunately, for the church, it was one of the greatest seasons ever. It was extremely difficult, and heavy, but God was faithful. In fact, the transition brought revival and great growth. Most of us back away from transitions, but like in childbirth, they are so healthy.

Many times, transition will cause people to press into God at a greater level. We need direction. We need wisdom. We finally declare, we need God. And God is so faithful to show up, and if we let him, bring beauty out of ashes.

Our church trusted God, and we transitioned from one church in a rural community, into four campuses in four different cities in English and Spanish.

What I learned is that you never get to where you are going if you are not willing to leave where you are. This is called transition. I want to challenge you as a leader to see the reward over the risk. Be led by faith, not fear. We often wonder what might go wrong in transition when we should wonder what could go right.

I have also learned in ministry that any time ministry is released into the hands of others, it is multiplied. This is demonstrated in the parable of the talents. When what we have is held onto is taken away. When what we have is released to others, it is multiplied.

In conclusion, if you want to see the beauty of other mountains, be willing to walk through the valleys of transition. They often feel like death, and in some ways they are. Some things must die for others to be born. For unless a seed is planted in the ground and dies, it can produce no fruit.

In transition, we often have to die to ourselves, our old ways, and the pride that we gained in the process. Transition can be like

Death Valley. We were made to pass through it but never live in it.

Yes, though you walk through the valley of the shadow of death, you will fear no evil. When you find yourself in the valley of transition, don't stop walking. Walk slower and with caution.

It takes some time to get through transition, but the day will come when the heaviness lifts and joy returns. When it does, it will be a glorious day. You will face transitions in your life, but if you will walk through them, you will see the glory of God on the other side.

Alan Latta, Senior Pastor, Generations Church, Granbury, Texas

What kept me hanging on? My most difficult season was when I was parking cars as a vocation and I never want to park cars again!

The determination developed in me by over eight years of parking cars made me never want to quit the ministry. Another thing that has helped me when under attack by flesh and blood people, is to pray this prayer. Lord, when have I treated someone like this? Please show me so I can repent.

I Thessalonians 16-18 "Rejoice always, pray without ceasing, in everything give thanks; for this is the will of God in Christ Jesus for you."

I have found that the Lord is able to do it so my own repentance and restoration can take place, which increases my enjoyment of His grace that is very much needed at the time.

D. Ray Miller

Pastoral, Minister, Various Churches for most of his life.

Only a few weeks after I became a pastor of my first church, I got this call. "Pastor, could you come before my wife, and I kill each other?" On the way I prayed and said, "Lord, not one teacher in the three Bible colleges I attended, told me what to do in a case like this." I was horribly unprepared for the battles. Soldiers are not made in classrooms, they're made in battles, by good leaders.

Our closest friends, who stopped by often to walk in the evenings, were offended because I did not approve of their son's homosexual lifestyle. They sent a petition to the church members to have us removed, put us through purgatory, and sent us down the road.

I loved being a pastor and preaching Jesus, leading souls to Christ, seeing people healed, and lives changed. I wish I could do it a couple more lifetimes. I loved it, but the intensity and extent of the battles were far beyond anything I ever imagined.

The impact on my wife and family was totally unexpected. I didn't know they would be a target in the middle of the battle.

Our oldest son was arrested on a Sunday morning and taken to jail for not showing up for court for a bill he had paid six weeks before. The fuel oil company forgot to notify the court. Our second son, (16 years old), was arrested and served four weekends in jail for not having a motorcycle endorsement on his driver's license. Do people go to jail for this?

The attorney looked me straight in the eye and said, "Reverend, what your daughter did is nothing, but because of who you are, it is going to be tough on your daughter!" My only daughter, (18 years old), was sentenced to 2-20 years in the penitentiary; not because of what she did, but because of what I did. I was a pastor who fought the powers of hell in our county.

I thought our youngest son had escaped the battle when we moved from that county. He was driving through, was stopped, his truck impounded, and told his license was expired. He and I went to the DMV, they apologized, said it was their mistake because he was in the system twice. No worry, they will correct it. Three weeks later, he was arrested and taken to jail. He spent four days in jail. The DMV forgot to correct their mistake and notify the court.

I'll always remember the day I was "done" as a pastor. My daughter was in jail, waiting to begin serving 2-20 years. My wife was in the hospital and didn't know me when I visited her. Also, our two sons, who had families to support, were out of work.

I was standing in our beautiful new church on five acres of land. Our congregation had grown from 66 to 350 in attendance. It looked like everything was wonderful; like I was a successful pastor, but I was done.

That day, I told the Lord I could not take one more step. I simply could not go on. I saw a long, black tunnel with very rough surfaces and there was no light at the end. Not even a lightning bug. I was everything you read in pastoral statistics. Totally devastated in the middle of a thriving church. I did not have one friend able to rescue me from devastation. I was as alone as a human could be.

I told God I couldn't preach another sermon. But I did. After shedding tears for hours, the next Sunday I preached under a powerful anointing. The Holy Spirit does that, in spite of our weakness.

During this episode, I wrote scriptures on copy paper and had them plastered all over the walls of my office. I would say again and again every day, "I will never give up Jesus." I constantly renewed my committed to God. I prayed continuously. My greatest fear was losing my mind.

I did not shed one tear in the presence of anyone. I wept alone, hours and days on end. A lady from Trinity Bible College in South Dakota was there with the Trinity Troubadours, a musical group. She asked how I was doing, and I said that I was fine. She came close, looked me in the eye and said, "No, you aren't! I know!"

Though I had never shed a tear in anyone's presence, at that moment I totally lost all my dignity and cried my heart out. She said, "God has this. Remember what you've preached all these years." I didn't believe her. I responded, "How many people do you know today that God has gotten out of jail?"

She was right.

My wife was miraculously healed and did seminars for women for emotional healing in three states. Our daughter was released after three weeks in the penitentiary to go to Christ for the Nations. After that, her record was expunged so she could go to nursing school. She has been a nurse for over 30 years.

Our two sons found plenty of carpentry work near Houston. I joined them and we worked together for a couple of years. We helped build a 3,000-car parking garage in Houston and remodeled a million-dollar house on a ranch west of Houston. It was a wonderful time we spent together as a family. No pressure, no demons to fight, just family.

And then I went back to pastoring. I went back into leading the fight against the forces of hell. I understand the call of God that cannot be hushed. It is who we are and the devil cannot change it. Being a pastor is the second hardest job on the earth. The hardest job is being a pastor's wife. Sometimes she must witness her children being mocked, she must remain silent and sweet because she is the pastor's wife.

Sometimes the people she struggles to tolerate demand more of her husband than she can, taking him away from his family and her. Family, church, community, and school, amount to a tremendous amount of pressure on a wife, mother, leader, and role model in the church. I did not realize how much pressure my wife lived under until she broke and collapsed completely under the emotional stress.

Pastors and ministry leaders, if you serve in ministry long, you too will have battle scars. Those who make it have made a job commitment. If it kills me, I will serve the Lord. We stay in ministry when there is nothing that can take us out.

My prayer is that the battles will make you and not break you and that you will become a stronger, more effective warrior for Jesus. This is a battle worth fighting. It is a battle worth winning. At the end of your journey may you be able to say with the Apostle Paul. "I have fought the good fight, I have finished the race, I have kept the faith." 2 Timothy 4:7

A *good fight* is the one you win!

APPENDIX

The Chronicles of Leroy (Meant to be humorous and memorable.)

By Pastor Nelson *Leroy* Coffman

Sweating bullets in prayer is never WASTED AMMUNITION.

What you lack in confidence make up for in dependence.

The greatest challenge of Christianity is not faith, but trust because trust is the proof of faith.

It's your faith that will move your mountains, but it's your trust that will carry you through your valley.

A church without a covering has a fuse lit and will eventually blow up.

Courage is the sail that catches the wind of your destiny.

Guilt can never escape the mind of God or man until freed by the one who forgives.

God's Word is the fountain of youth people seldom drink from.

The church is a melting pot of personalities we fondue together.

Each tick of God's clock is a test for God's people.

Death always produces life at a funeral if the pastor will open the coffin and give opportunity for people to get out.

Tattoos are the graffiti written on the walls of God's temple.

A girl is often the favorite candy Satan sells to those willing to pay the price.

Faith tests are best taken with a dose of communion, a script from the Great Physician and plenty of rest from your burden.

Prophetic words are seeds sown that are watered by the Word, fertilized by the Spirit, and grown into maturity by faith.

Moral decisions lead to divine destinations; immoral decisions lead to demonic devastation.

When you get to your wits end, you will find God lives there.

Adversity is God's way of building a closer relationship with you.

If you are not praying in the Spirit, you have a chink in your armor.

Your success is not the size of your flock, but it's spiritual health.

The success of an oak tree is not in its roots but in the acorn.

You can't do anything about what you can't do anything about! So why stress out?

Prayer is the gift wrapping the anointing comes in.

Faith is the fearful man's courage.

Love is determined by the depth of your efforts not the shallowness of your words.

Revelation of the Holy Spirit is the deep water we swim in that others can drink from.

Ministry can be a juggling act in this circus we call life.

Naked devils are no match for those wearing God's armor.

The five temptations for every minister: Glory, Gold, Girls, Guys, Gluttony.

You know you have forgiven someone when you're driving down the road and you see that person pullover by the highway patrol, getting a ticket, and you don't laugh!

Pastors are in the people business because people last forever!

Answering the call to ministry is a wonderful conversation until you hang up!

ABOUT THE AUTHOR

Pastor Nelson Coffman attended Northeast Texas Bible College and graduated from Christ For the Nations Institute in Dallas, TX. He has served in pastoral ministry for 36 years and is currently serving as the Founding Pastor of Harvest Hill Church in Midlothian, TX. He has raised up many leaders and has a passion to help people come into the fullness of God's purpose and destiny for their lives.

He has a heart to help pastors and ministry leaders survive the difficult seasons of ministry. Pastor Nelson has been married to Karen since 1975 and they have 3 grown children who are all serving the Lord in the work of the ministry. They also have 9 amazing grandchildren.